Transmaterial 2

Transmaterial 2

EDITED BY
BLAINE BROWNELL

Transmaterial 2

A CATALOG
OF MATERIALS
THAT
REDEFINE
OUR
PHYSICAL
ENVIRONMENT

PRINCETON ARCHITECTURAL PRESS
NEW YORK

TO MY PARENTS

Published by
Princeton Architectural Press
37 East Seventh Street
New York, New York 10003

For a free catalog of books, call 1.800.722.6657.
Visit our website at www.papress.com.

Editing: Linda Lee
Design: Paul Wagner

Special thanks to: Nettie Aljian, Sara Bader, Dorothy Ball,
Nicola Bednarek, Janet Behning, Kristin Carlson,
Becca Casbon, Penny (Yuen Pik) Chu, Russell Fernandez,
Pete Fitzpatrick, Wendy Fuller, Jan Haux, Clare Jacobson,
John King, Nancy Eklund Later, Laurie Manfra,
Katharine Myers, Lauren Nelson Packard,
Jennifer Thompson, Arnoud Verhaeghe, Joseph Weston,
and Deb Wood of Princeton Architectural Press
—Kevin C. Lippert, publisher

Library of Congress Cataloging-in-Publication Data
Transmaterial 2 : a catalog of materials that redefine our
physical environment / edited by Blaine Brownell. — 1st ed.
        p.   cm.
Includes indexes.
ISBN 978-1-56898-722-4 (pbk. : alk. paper)
1. Materials—Technological innovations. 2. Materials—
Catalogs. I. Brownell, Blaine Erickson, 1970– II. Title:
Transmaterial two.
TA403.6.T15 2008
620.1'1—dc22
                              2007022126

TABLE OF CONTENTS

Approximately two years after the publication of *Transmaterial 1*, we live in a climate in which the effects of significant material change in the physical environment are becoming evident. Alternative-energy technologies, resource-conservation measures, and pollution-reduction strategies are transforming the way buildings and products are made. New digital technologies are facilitating fabrication and reintroducing sophisticated craft-making capabilities in construction. A recent interest in biomimicry has led to a generation of prototypes based on cellular, algorithmically generated forms based on the active study of living structures. We have entered a new era, and the rules are still unclear. However, the change is palpable.

Transmaterial 1 presented the design-materials revolution in its nascent phase. Changes that transpired during the subsequent two years recommend the reevaluation of assumptions addressed in the first book, which described the steady progress of technology, the adoption of aerospace and military inventions for the consumer market, increasing environmental awareness, and interest in phenomenological effects as the primary motivators for material innovation. Although these factors remain important motivators today, it is important to reorder them based on updated priorities. The bulk of new material development at the turn of the century was the result of the steady progress of technology; the primary motivators now are environmental concerns. This fundamental change means that virtually every material, product, and building-system manufacturer is developing new technologies and revising existing ones in order to accommodate the recent surge of interest in environmental awareness and "green building."

MOTIVATIONS 2.0

Nearly a decade into the twenty-first century, the optimism ushered in by the new millennium has been overshadowed by new anxieties regarding global environmental and political instabilities. Global warming is of paramount concern, frequently addressed in headline news by the international media. Although it remains difficult to predict exactly how the influence of anthropogenic emissions will ultimately affect the environment, recent studies indicate acceleration in the changes brought about by the atmospheric accumulation of greenhouse gases. Not only are CO_2 emissions under increased scrutiny but also ozone, perfluorochemicals, and other pervasive pollutants. Materials that release volatile organic compounds (VOCs) and contribute to unhealthy indoor air quality, or "sick building syndrome," are likewise being evaluated. As a result, manufacturers have become serious about developing nontoxic and low-VOC products, as well as less-polluting alternatives by which to manufacture them. Photocatalysis has also been embraced as a means to reduce air pollution, exemplified by the use of titanium dioxide in self-cleaning coatings.

While the adverse effects of greenhouse gases and pollution are not immediately visible, natural and human-made disasters provide cause for immediate concern. The Asian Tsunami and Hurricane Katrina, for example, emphasized the extent of destruction that nature can bring about; 9/11, the Iraq war, and increasing instability within impoverished nations have contributed to a general feeling of insecurity. This sense of vulnerability has resulted in a recent increase in the number of security-related products, such as building panels that provide increased resistance against storms and ballistic loads and sophisticated electronic detection-and-alert systems.

Energy is another topic strongly related to issues of global insecurity. "Peak oil," a theme largely confined to conversations within a small scientific community a few years ago, has since come to dominate discussions among environmentalists and big oil companies alike. There is now strong consensus that the increasing demand for petroleum will outpace supply within the next quarter century. Because of the extent to which petroleum-based sources are utilized for energy, transportation, manufacturing, polymers, agriculture, and other applications, a serious effort is now underway to develop alternative fuels to mitigate the negative effects of peak oil. Governments, utilities, and corporations worldwide have increased investments in rapidly renewable power generation and raised energy-conservation standards. New light-piping technologies and improved insulation materials enhance building performance while saving energy. Manufacturing is increasingly deployed at the location of use in order to reduce transportation costs, and companies are pursuing regional production capabilities at building sites as a result. Rapidly renewable materials are also replacing fossil fuel–based sources in products like food containers, packaging, and mobile electronic devices.

As the depletion of material resources continues, product manufacturers must be more creative about how to optimize raw materials and utilize waste. Conventional materials are enhanced with augmented dimensionality for additional strength and elongated spans; exotic new fibers and composites exhibit increased strength-to-weight ratios. The more frequent use of waste materials in manufacturing new products has helped alter the perception of recycling—no longer viewed as having downgraded value. In many cases, products diverted from the waste stream are converted into uses that exhibit greater value than their original applications. Rapidly renewable materials are replacing old-growth sources, and rapid-growth plants are being scrutinized for their value as fuels or other material replacements.

One of the most interesting developments in the world of materials is dematerialization. The evolution of technology has inevitably accounted for the limited availability of resources, and in the fabrication of new products, manufacturers have spread valuable minerals, polymers, and fibers across greater possible spans than previously imaginable, producing products with equal or greater utility with significantly less raw material. The new versions also integrate lesser-value substances, such as adhesives, fillers, and air, to further extend their usefulness. The resulting products not only use less material but are often lighter, stronger, and more stable. This trend leads to interesting new hybrids as well as products with increased porosity and light transmittance. Translucency becomes increasingly appreciated for its own aesthetic merit, and in a few cases conventionally opaque and solid materials, like concrete, are being modified to transmit light. This development parallels the outgrowth of value placed on the provocative aspects associated with rendering standard conventions obsolete.

Not only has technology allowed us to do more with less, it has also provided the tools to manipulate materials more extensively for less cost. During the twentieth century, large-scale industrial processes that emphasized standardization largely displaced the craftsperson. Detailed material manipulation and ornamentation became increasingly rare and costly. The advent of digital fabrication technologies has reintroduced the detailed individual artistry and sophisticated material refinement of the craftsperson. Most notably, new tools tend to shift control over the final product from the hands of the builder to those of the designer, allowing a variety of unprecedented capabilities such as image-based topographies and algorithmically derived surfaces. One outcome of this trend is the "Photoshop effect," in which graphical content conceived within the computer is directly applied to the physical surfaces of products, buildings, and landscapes.

The industrial era gave birth to mass production and product quantity but also ushered in homogenization. Globalization, likewise, disrupts local customs and idiosyncratic processes in favor of the universal, where product quality is largely defined by predictability, consistency, and uniformity. An increasing number of manufacturers participate in a counter trend in which materials exhibit unique characteristics based on contextual needs. Mass-customized, responsive, and/or interactive products, such as shape memory polymers, photoluminescent surfaces, or expandable furniture, shape environments that correlate more directly with specific contexts as well as transform based on varying needs. Smart materials also provide unprecedented feedback enhancements, from monitoring bodily health to signaling environmental quality levels.

TRENDS

As established in the first volume, several broad categories serve to elucidate current material transformations. These classifications highlight important themes shared between dissimilar products and make unexpected connections. For example, an aluminum floor system and polypropylene chair are made of different substances, but they could be similarly important in their use of recycled materials. The seven broad categories I have proposed are as follows:

1. ULTRAPERFORMING

Throughout human history, material innovation has been defined by the persistent testing of limits. Ultraperforming materials are stronger, lighter, more durable, and more flexible than their conventional counterparts. These materials are important because they shatter known boundaries and necessitate new thinking about the shaping of our physical environment.

As discussed above, the ongoing pursuit of thinner, more porous, and less-opaque products indicates a notable movement toward greater exposure and ephemerality. It is no surprise that ultraperforming materials are generally expensive and difficult to obtain, although many of these products are being developed for a broad market.

2. MULTIDIMENSIONAL

Materials are physically defined by three dimensions, but many products have long been conceived as flat surfaces. A new trend exploits the z-axis in the manufacture of a wide variety of materials for various uses, ranging from fabrics to wall and ceiling treatments. Greater depth allows thin materials to become more structurally stable, and materials with enhanced texture and richness are often more visually interesting. Augmented dimensionality will likely continue to be a growing movement, especially considering the technological trends toward miniaturization, systems integration, and prefabrication.

3. REPURPOSED

Repurposed materials may be defined as surrogates, or materials that are used in the place of materials conventionally used in an application. Repurposed materials provide several benefits, such as replacing precious raw materials with less-endangered, more plentiful ones; diverting products from the waste stream; implementing less-toxic manufacturing processes; and defying convention. A subset of this group comprises objects considered repurposed in terms of their functionality, such as tables that become light sources and art that becomes furniture.

As a trend, repurposing underscores the desire for adaptability and an increasing awareness of our limited resources. While the performance of repurposed materials is not always identical to that of the products they replace, sometimes new and unexpected benefits arise from their use.

4. RECOMBINANT

Recombinant materials consist of two or more different materials that act in harmony to create a product that performs greater than the sum of its parts. Such hybrids are created when inexpensive or recyclable products are used as filler, when a combination allows for the achievement of multiple functions, when a precious resource may be emulated by combining less-precious materials, or when different materials act in symbiosis to exhibit high-performance characteristics.

Recombinant materials have long proven their performance in the construction industry. Reinforced concrete, which benefits from the compressive strength and fireproof qualities of concrete and the tensile strength of steel, is a classic recombination. These materials are often composed of down-cycled components, which may be difficult if not impossible to re-extract, and the success of recombinant materials is based on their reliable integration, which is not always predictable. However, the continued value exhibited by many such hybrids is evidence of its growing popularity.

5. INTELLIGENT

Intelligent is a catchall term for materials that are designed to improve their environment and that often take inspiration from biological systems. They can act actively or passively and can be high- or low-tech. Many materials in this category indicate a focus on the manipulation of the microscopic scale.

Intelligence is not used here to describe products that have autonomous computational power but rather products that are inherently smart by design. The varied list of benefits provided by these materials includes pollution reduction, water purification, solar-radiation control, natural ventilation, and power generation. An intelligent product may simply be a flexible or modular system that adds value throughout its life cycle.

6. TRANSFORMATIONAL

Transformational materials undergo a physical metamorphosis based on environmental stimuli. This change may occur automatically based on the inherent properties of the material, or it may be user driven. Like intelligent materials, transformational materials provide a variety of benefits, including waste reduction, enhanced ergonomics, solar control, illumination, as well as unique phenomenological effects. Transformational products offer multiple functions where one would be expected, provide benefits that few might have imagined, and help us view the world differently.

7. INTERFACIAL

The interface has been a popular design focus since the birth of the digital age. Interfacial materials, products, and systems navigate between the physical and virtual realms. As we spend greater amounts of time interacting with computer-based tools and environments, the bridges that facilitate the interaction between the two worlds are subject to further scrutiny.

So-called interfacial products may be virtual instruments that control material manufacture or physical manifestations of digital fabrications. These tools provide unprecedented and unimaginable capabilities, such as enhanced technology-infused work environments, rapid-prototyping of complex shapes, integration of digital imagery within physical objects, and making the invisible visible.

Interfacial materials employ the latest computing and communications technologies and suggest society's future trajectory. Interfacial materials are not infallible, but they expand our capabilities into uncharted territory.

ONWARD

Inspired by environmental imperatives, new technologies, and unprecedented design opportunities, the design and construction industries are undergoing an extraordinary transformation. The conservatism that once characterized the construction trade is melting away, and innovation is spreading with an increased sense of ecological responsibility, measurable performance enhancement, and enhanced brand differentiation..

As this volume hopefully demonstrates, *Transmaterial* is a living, evolving project with a few simple goals: heighten awareness about new materials and technologies, provide tools to access and use these materials and technologies, and affect positive change via enhanced design and construction. As the subscriber list to the weekly product emails continues to grow, a fascinating community of material manufacturers, designers, artists, scientists, architects, builders, students, and engineers has evolved to recommend, assess, and test new products. Please visit www.transmaterial.net as well as the website of Princeton Architectural Press's companion program, *Materials Monthly*, at www.materialsmonthly.com, where you may continue to discover exciting developments in the world of materials beyond those contained within this collection.

Blaine Brownell

A

Blob Wall

B

Nº 066000-012

D

Rubber

C

FREE-STANDING MODULAR WALL SYSTEM

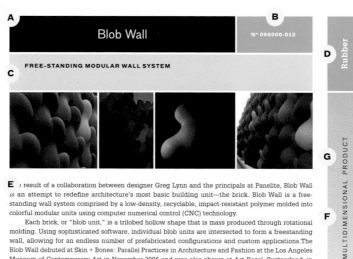

G

F

MULTIDIMENSIONAL PRODUCT

E e result of a collaboration between designer Greg Lynn and the principals at Panelite, Blob Wall is an attempt to redefine architecture's most basic building unit—the brick. Blob Wall is a free-standing wall system comprised by a low-density, recyclable, impact-resistant polymer molded into colorful modular units using computer numerical control (CNC) technology.

Each brick, or "blob unit," is a trilobed hollow shape that is mass produced through rotational molding. Using sophisticated software, individual blob units are intersected to form a freestanding wall, allowing for an endless number of prefabricated configurations and custom applications.The Blob Wall debuted at Skin + Bones: Parallel Practices in Architecture and Fashion at the Los Angeles Museum of Contemporary Art in November 2006 and was also shown at Art Basel, Switzerland, in June 2007.

H CONTENTS
Linear low-density
polyethylene (LLDPE)

APPLICATIONS
Spatial divider or sculptural
installation for exterior or
interior applications

TYPES / SIZES
6 standard designs, 6 color
schemes; 18'–7" x 2'–3" x 9'
(5.7 x .7 x 2.7 m); custom
wall configurations
and color combinations
available

ENVIRONMENTAL
Recyclable, may be
produced using recycled
material (dark colors only),
efficient use of material:
wall thickness is 1/8"
(.32 cm)

LIMITATIONS
Not fire-rated, not intended
for load-bearing
applications

CONTACT
Panelite
5835 Adams Boulevard
Culver City, CA 90232
Tel: 323-297-0115
www.panelite.us
blobwall@panelite.us

A. NAME

The trademarked name of the particular entry being featured

B. NUMBER (Nº)

This nine-digit identification number is unique to each entry. The first six digits are based on the new MasterFormat material classification system, published June 8, 2004, by the Construction Specifications Institute. The last three digits are used to identify each product within a serial list. This numbering system is congruent with the *Materials Monthly* program, also published by Princeton Architectural Press.

C. DESCRIPTION

A brief, generic explanation of each entry

D. CATEGORY

Refers to the basic materiality of the product, such as concrete, metal, or plastic; it is the primary means of organization in this book.

E. SUMMARY

A basic text description of each entry

F. TREND

This field assigns one of the seven trends mentioned in the introduction to each entry: ultraperforming, multidimensional, repurposed, recombinant, intelligent, transformational, or interfacial.

G. TYPE

Defines each entry as a material, product, or process

H. ADDITIONAL DATA

The following information is also used to describe product entries: contents, applications, types or sizes, environmental benefits, industry tests or examinations, limitations, and manufacturer contact information.

01: **CONCRETE**

CarbonCast

PRECAST CONCRETE WITH CARBON-FIBER-GRID REINFORCEMENT

CarbonCast is a precast-concrete technology that uses a carbon-fiber grid for secondary reinforcing or shear transfer, depending on the application. Because carbon-fiber reinforcing resists corrosion, CarbonCast precast products require less concrete cover, resulting in added durability, lighter weight, and improved sustainability over traditional precast concrete. In addition, the reduction of concrete enables the integration of insulation, which can increase R-values of wall panels.

CarbonCast architectural cladding panels can weigh up to 66 percent less than conventional precast panels. This weight reduction permits engineers to reduce substructure or specify smaller cranes for lifting the panels into place. When used in the flanges of CarbonCast pretopped double tees, the carbon-fiber grid can reduce weight by 12 percent and eliminate the need for sealers and sacrificial barrier coatings. When used as a shear connector in CarbonCast high-performance insulated wall panels, the carbon-fiber grid improves thermal performance, given its relatively low thermal conductivity.

CONTENTS
Precast concrete, carbon fiber

APPLICATIONS
Load-bearing and non-load-bearing exterior walls, slabs

TYPES / SIZES
Architectural cladding panels, high performance insulated wall panels, pretopped double tees, residential wall panels, and stem decks (size dependent on design)

ENVIRONMENTAL
Carbon fiber is corrosion resistant, requires less concrete cover, and can enable improved R-values

TESTS / EXAMINATIONS
Extensive material characterization of carbon-fiber grids (modified ASTM D3039) and full-scale product testing, including ASTM E119 fire tests

CONTACT
Altus Precast
PO Box 10097
Lancaster, PA 17605
Tel: 1-866-GO-ALTUS
www.altusprecast.com
info@altusprecast.com

Chronos Chromos Concrete

DYNAMIC INFORMATION DISPLAY WITHIN CONCRETE SURFACES

Chris Glaister, Afshin Mehin, and Tomas Rosen developed Chronos Chromos Concrete in order to animate a ubiquitous material. Intrigued by the fact that concrete structures tend to age, discolor, and degrade over a period of decades, the designers came up with the idea of integrating thermochromatic pigment and timekeeping devices within a concrete matrix in order to make the material more dynamic and engaging.

In their first prototype clock, a band of white travels smoothly across an undulating dark gray surface once per minute. A digital display of minutes and hours is represented by a series of constant white lines.

Since winning first prize in the BCA concrete creativity awards, Chronos Chromos Concrete has been crafted into clocks for the home and office and is currently being developed as a 40 x 78 inch (100 x 200 centimeter) dot-matrix information display for the entrance hall of a new building in London.

CONTENTS

Cement, limestone aggregates, glass fibers, thermochromatic pigment

APPLICATIONS

Anything from home products to large-scale architectural installations; sealed structural information displays such as clocks and dot-matrix displays

TYPES / SIZES

Pixels from .03 to .15 in^2 (.20 to 1 cm^2) can be produced and repeated up to any size requirement

LIMITATIONS

Sensitive to ambient temperature

CONTACT

Chromastone UK
Innovation RCA
Kensington Gore
London SW7 2EU
United Kingdom
Tel: +44 (0)7971-073-129
www.chromastone.com
info@chromastone.com

Concrete Canvas Shelter

RAPIDLY DEPLOYABLE BUILDING MADE FROM CONCRETE CLOTH

The Concrete Canvas Shelter is a rapidly deployable hardened shelter that requires only water and air for erection. It can be deployed by two people without any training in approximately thirty minutes and is ready to use in twelve hours. The shelter consists of a cement-impregnated fabric (Concrete Cloth) bonded to the outer surface of an inflatable plastic inner structure.

Prior to construction, the shelter is delivered folded in a sealed plastic sack. Once the sack is positioned and filled with water, the fiber matrix wicks water into the cement, naturally controlling the water-to-cement ratio. The sack is cut open after hydration, and a battery-driven fan inflates the inner plastic lining, causing the structure to lift. After a duration of twelve hours, the concrete will have set sufficiently for use.

The fibers of the Concrete Canvas fabric form a coherent matrix within the concrete, providing tensile reinforcement and helping prevent crack propagation. If desired, the shelter can be buried with over 20 inches (50 centimeters) of sand on the roof in order to provide increased insulation and protection.

CONTENTS
Concrete

APPLICATIONS
Emergency shelter, ground improvement, helipads, building repairs, damp proofing, formwork, fire protection

TYPES / SIZES
172.2 ft^2 and 269.1 ft^2
(16 m^2) and 25 m^2) area

ENVIRONMENTAL
Rapid deployment of shelter for emergency aid, efficient use of material, good thermal properties

LIMITATIONS
Setup time is 30 minutes, but sufficient hardening requires 12 hours

CONTACT
Peter Brewin
Wpack Industrial
Estate Road
Northampton NN7 2NJ
United Kingdom
Tel: +44 (0)1604-864-630
www.concretecanvas.co.uk
info@concretecanvas.co.uk

EcoX

FIBER-REINFORCED 100%-RECYCLED-GLASS PRECAST CONCRETE

According to Meld, over seven million tons of glass are sent to landfills each year in the United States alone. EcoX is precast concrete made of about 75 percent postconsumer and postindustrial glass. It may be used for countertops, furniture, fixtures, sculptural objects, and nonstructural applications. With its high volume of recycled glass content, EcoX appears markedly different from conventional precast concrete and diverts useful material from the waste stream.

CONTENTS
Portland cement, glass pozzolan, recycled-container glass, alkaline-stable pigments, fibers

APPLICATIONS
Furniture, tiles, countertops, site objects, wall panels, sinks, art objects

TYPES / SIZES
Custom

ENVIRONMENTAL
100% recycled postconsumer and postindustrial glass, recyclable

LIMITATIONS
Not structural

CONTACT
Meld
3001-103 Spring
Forest Road
Raleigh, NC 27616
Tel: 919-790-1749
www.meldusa.com
info@meldusa.com

Eterno Luminoso and Lumineo

N° 096613-001

PHOTOLUMINESCENT AND FLUORESCENT TERRAZZO

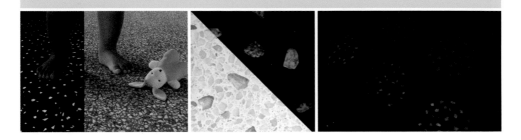

Eterno Luminoso and Eterno Lumineo add luminescence to terrazzo flooring. Specially treated, masked aggregates can be evenly distributed over the surface or grouped in patterns, like circles, lines, or arrows, and can provide safety features in the dark or striking effects under black light.

Under normal light conditions, Eterno Luminoso and Eterno Lumineo are similar in appearance to traditional terrazzo floors. Eterno Luminoso combines the durability of terrazzo with functional and decorative photoluminescent after-glow effects. While traditional floor safety markings are obtrusive, this material's luminance complies with the concept of "hidden safety," referring to an autonomously operating, reliable evacuation-guidance system that is noticeable only during light failure. Eterno Luminoso may enhance evacuations and mitigate panic, particularly in buildings where emergency exits may not be obvious.

Eterno Lumineo utilizes fluorescence, revealing bright light effects when illuminated by backlight. It is available in multiple colors and is also appropriate for decorative purposes in theaters, discotheques, or cinemas.

CONTENTS
Concrete and (luminescent) aggregates

APPLICATIONS
Flooring in commercial, institutional, and infrastructural projects

TYPES / SIZES
Custom

ENVIRONMENTAL
100% recyclable

TESTS / EXAMINATIONS
NTA 7909, DIN 51130

LIMITATIONS
Application depends on subsurface structure

CONTACT
Eterno Terrazzo BV
Hefbrugweg 26B
1332 AP Almere, Flevoland
The Netherlands
Tel: + 31 (0)36-532-9877
www.eternoterrazzo.nl
info@eternoterrazzo.nl

Extablemeconcrete

FIBER-REINFORCED PRECAST CONCRETE

Extremeconcrete is a hyper-reinforced concrete that has the density of stone without the heavy weight. Meld's proprietary reinforcement process distributes two types of fiber throughout the product for added strength and durability, creating a three-dimensional backbone to help maintain surface integrity. This blend of fibers creates a distinctive texture that reveals visual depth in the finished material.

Because of its superior density, Extremeconcrete can be poured into a broad array of custom forms for interior or exterior use. In modular or monolithic pours, the product is designed to be hand cast and finished. Meld has also developed a special sealing and polishing process to help protect the material.

CONTENTS
Portland cement/pozzolan, silica sand, alkaline-stable pigments, fibers, high-performance concrete admixtures/fillers

APPLICATIONS
Furniture, tiles, countertops, site objects, wall panels, sinks, art objects

TYPES / SIZES
Custom

ENVIRONMENTAL
Recyclable

LIMITATIONS
Not structural

CONTACT
Meld
3001-103 Spring
Forest Road
Raleigh, NC 27616
Tel: 919-790-1749
www.meldusa.com
info@meldusa.com

Graphic Concrete

PATTERNED PRECAST CONCRETE

Graphic Concrete offers a new way to produce a patterned concrete surface. Graphic Concrete's patented technology involves the application of a surface retarder to the exterior of a concrete form-liner. This method allows precast-concrete manufacturers to produce high-quality concrete elements, panels, and slabs. The end result is a patterned, smooth, or completely exposed surface. The pattern on the surface comes from from the contrast between the smooth face and the exposed fine aggregate finish in the concrete.

Designers may select patterns from the GCCollection or develop their own designs using GCPro custom design software. The concrete surface can also be even, in which case the options are smooth and velvety (GCSmooth) or a completely exposed fine aggregate finish (GCExpose). Graphic Concrete is suitable for facades, panels, partition walls, and garden slabs.

CONTENTS
Concrete, surface-retarder membrane

APPLICATIONS
Concrete facades, architectural panels, partitions, garden walls, slabs

TYPES / SIZES
Custom (unlimited sizes)

ENVIRONMENTAL
Reduced need for solvents, reduced dust problems, reduced retarder concentration in cleaning agent

LIMITATIONS
Not for cast-in-place applications

CONTACT
Graphic Concrete Ltd.
Porkkalankatu 11 H 11
00180 Helsinki
Finland
Tel: +358 9-6842-0093
www.graphicconcrete.com
info@graphicconcrete.fi

Litracon

LIGHT-TRANSMITTING CONCRETE

Litracon, a light-transmitting concrete developed by Hungarian architect Áron Losonczi, evoked a tremendous response within the international design community at the time of its unveiling. A combination of optical fibers and fine concrete, Litracon may be produced in panel form as well as prefabricated building blocks. The large number and small diameter of the light-transmitting fibers result in a homogeneous mixture that assumes a new identity. Part structural concrete, part light-transmissive surface, Litracon immediately calls into question known conventions of both materials.

Load-bearing walls may be constructed using Litracon, as the glass fibers act as an aggregate and have no adverse effect on the strength of the concrete. Despite their relatively small proportion—only 4 percent of the total volume of the blocks—the parallel optical fibers transmit light effectively through walls up to several meters thick. Shadows conveyed through the material are rendered crisply, and the light color is unchanged.

CONTENTS
96% concrete, 4% optical fiber

APPLICATIONS
Exterior or interior light-transmitting walls, shading devices, illuminated paving, light fixtures, signage

TYPES / SIZES
Gray, black, or white; layered or organic fiber distribution patterns; block size 23 5/8 x 11 13/16" (60 x 30 cm), 1 to 19 11/16" (2.5 to 50 cm) thick

CONTACT
Litracon
Bt Tanya 832
6640 Csongrád
Hungary
Tel: +36 30-255-1648
www.litracon.hu
info@litracon.hu

Reckli Formliners

TEXTURING SYSTEM FOR EXPOSED-CONCRETE SURFACES

While fabrication of textured exposed-concrete surfaces using elastic formliners has been practiced worldwide for more than thirty-five years, Reckli Formliners offer a significant improvement. Made from an elastic polyurethane, the formliners allow the release of the formliner from the concrete without damage to the concrete or the formliner itself. Reckli Formliners can be used for precast as well as cast-in-place concrete.

There are five different possibilities for the application: standard formliners with about two hundred standard patterns, one-off formliners for custom designs, photo-engraving formliners that allow for the transfer of photographic images, one-time formliners for single-use applications, and liquid compounds for make-your-own formliners.

CONTENTS
Polyurethane elastomers

APPLICATIONS
Precast or cast-in-place concrete

TYPES / SIZES
Custom

ENVIRONMENTAL
Waste reduction (high reusability)

TESTS / EXAMINATIONS
Shore hardness, concrete resistance, tear resistance

LIMITATIONS
50 to 100 reuses

CONTACT
Reckli-Chemiewerkstoff GmbH
Eschstr. 30
44629 Herne, NRW
Germany
Tel: +49 2323-1706-0
www.reckli.de
info@reckli.de

Superabsorber

SOUND-, LIGHT-, AND AIR-POLLUTION-ABSORBING HIGHWAY BARRIER SYSTEM

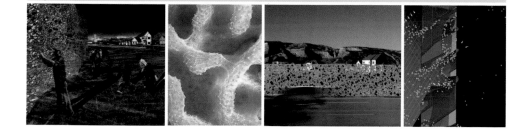

In the United States there are over 46,800 miles (75,317 kilometers) of highways with sound-barrier walls being erected daily to mitigate the negative impacts of highway systems on adjacent neighborhoods. The increasing prominence of this addition to the highway infrastructure necessitates a more appealing design solution to highway-generated air, sound, and light pollution.

In addition to mitigating sound and light pollution, the Superabsorber system also absorbs airborne pollutants. (Transportation systems alone produce 1.4 billion tons of airborne pollution annually.) Designed by Douglas Hecker and Martha Skinner of Clemson-based fieldoffice, this innovative system has the potential to significantly reduce airborne pollution with the application of photocatalytic cement products that have been demonstrated to reduce air pollution in urban areas by 50 percent when covering just 15 percent of urban surfaces. The inclusion of this surface application on future concrete-barrier systems will produce a significant increase in absorption of air pollution in urban areas.

CONTENTS
Photocatalytic cement with high-volume fly ash, glass-fiber reinforcing

APPLICATIONS
Highway barrier system, environmentally improving spatial divider

TYPES / SIZES
10 x 35' (3 x 10.7 m) panels

ENVIRONMENTAL
Mitigates air, sound, and light pollution

CONTACT
fieldoffice
272 Riggs Drive
Clemson, SC 29631
Tel: 864-653-5025
www.field-office.com
info@field-office.com

TX Active

POLLUTION-REDUCING CEMENT

TX Active is a photocatalytic cement developed by Italcementi. It decreases the harmful substances present in the air as well as preserves the finished surface of buildings. Incorporating titanium dioxide as its active ingredient, the cement reduces concentrations of airborne pollutants, such as nitrogen oxides and volatile organic compounds.

The TX Active product line consists of two different hydraulic binders: TX Aria and TX Arca. TX Aria is a binder for paints, mortars and leveling compounds, plasters and coatings, as well as concrete. TX Arca is a cement specifically designed for high-profile architectural works, and it complies with European Standard EN 197/1 requirements. Concrete made with TX Arca cement has the same physical and mechanical properties as traditional concrete, with the added self-cleaning properties of TX Active.

CONTENTS
Photocatalytic hydraulic binder

APPLICATIONS
Interior and exterior vertical and horizontal surfaces

TYPES / SIZES
TX Aria, TX Arca

ENVIRONMENTAL
Reduces air pollution, reduces maintenance

TESTS / EXAMINATIONS
European Standard EN 197/1; other certifications available on request

CONTACT
Italcementi
Via G. Camozzi, 124
BG 24121 Bergamo
Italy
Tel: +39 (0)35-396-111
www.italcementigroup.com
txactive@itcgr.net

ILLUMINATED CONCRETE-AND-GLASS FLOOR

Underlit Flooring is a polished concrete-and-glass flooring system suitable for interior applications, such as kitchens and bathrooms, and various external applications, including gardens and terraces. Available by the square meter and in custom sizes and colors, the concrete tiles can be laid directly onto an existing floor. The glass lenses are lit by fiber optics laid directly under the tiles and powered by a single bulb that will effectively illuminate areas up to 1,076 square feet (100 square meters). The color of the light can be altered at the touch of a button or left to change automatically over a period of time, creating a subtly shifting ambiance. Underlit Flooring may also be installed as a wall cladding system.

CONTENTS
Reinforced concrete, glass, fiber optics

APPLICATIONS
Flooring and wall cladding

TYPES / SIZES
Various sizes and custom shapes

ENVIRONMENTAL
Made from 60% recycled materials

CONTACT
Concrete Blond
140 Victoria Park Road
London E9 7JN
United Kingdom
Tel: +44 (0)7989-225-586
www.concrete-blond.com
info@concrete-blond.com

Walled Paper

CONCRETE CLADDING WITH DECORATIVE RELIEF

From a distance Walled Paper appears to be typical applied patterned paper, but it is a concrete panel with a pattern cast into its surface with a textural depth of 1/64 to 3/16 inches (.03 to .5 centimeters). Combining the raw effect of concrete with the decorative effect of wallpaper and other fine patterning, Walled Paper is appropriate for use in applications ranging from internal and external cladding systems to floors and surfaces. At its finest casting depth the effect is barely distinguishable from wallpaper, imparting a subtle satinlike pattern to this most industrial of materials. Available in Brutalist gray concrete, in Victoriana black, or Portland white, the lightweight panels can be adapted to most architectural attachment and cladding mechanisms or employed as standalone panels.

CONTENTS
Concrete

APPLICATIONS
Wall cladding

TYPES / SIZES
Various sizes and custom shapes

ENVIRONMENTAL
Made from 60% recycled materials

CONTACT
Concrete Blond
140 Victoria Park Road
London E9 7JN
United Kingdom
Tel: +44 (0)7989-225-586
www.concrete-blond.com
info@concrete-blond.com

02: **MINERAL**

Fusionstone

FUSED STONE-AND-PROTECTIVE-GLASS COMPOSITE

The Fusionstone proprietary process involves ultra-clear glass permanently fused to exotic stone slabs to achieve superior surface protection while retaining and showcasing the beauty of natural stone. It eliminates adhesion lines, and the material appears entirely translucent from edge to edge. As a result, natural stone can be used in applications where it was once prohibited because intrusion of natural and chemical substances into porous marbles, sandstones, and limestones is completely prevented. LED lighting can also be integrated into Fusionstone for additional aesthetic enhancement.

CONTENTS
Stone, glass

APPLICATIONS
Counter surfaces, flooring

TYPES / SIZES
Custom fabrication of
shapes and edging

CONTACT
Architectural Systems Inc.
150 West 25th Street
8th Floor
New York, NY 10001
Tel: 212-206-1730
www.archsystems.com
sales@archsystems.com

HIGH-RELIEF CERAMIC FORMS

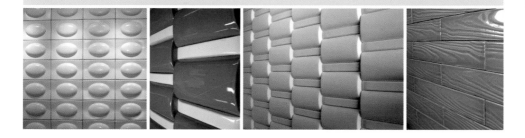

Kerrigan ceramic architectural tiles are the result of Chicago-based designer Bryan Kerrigan's methodical exploration of the dimensionality and texture of ceramic tile. Designed and manufactured using high-temperature-fired stoneware clay, the tiles are very durable for both interior and exterior applications in all climates.

Beginning his work with ceramics in the early nineties, Kerrigan developed pottery and sculpture with fluid, organic shapes. His experiments in ceramic art led to the development of hand-sculpted tiles for architectural applications. Noting the extent to which the subtlest alterations of plan and edge affected the dimension of the forms, Kerrigan embarked upon several years of thorough ceramics research in order to produce his current collection.

MULTIDIMENSIONAL PRODUCT

CONTENTS
Clay, glaze

APPLICATIONS
Interior and exterior wall, floor, and ceiling coverings

TYPES / SIZES
Oval form 14 1/2 x 9 x 1 7/8" (36.8 x 22.9 x 4.8 cm), large weave form 15 1/4 x 8 x 1 7/8" (38.7 x 20.3 x 4.8 cm) or 15 1/4 x 2 5/8 x 1" (38.7 x 6.7 x 2.5 cm), wood grain form 27 x 4 1/2 x 3/4" (68.6 x 11.4 x 1.9 cm)

ENVIRONMENTAL
Plentiful resource, nonmold harboring

TESTS / EXAMINATIONS
EPA 15 U.S. C.2604

CONTACT
Bryan Kerrigan
457 North Racine Avenue
Chicago, IL 60622
Tel: 312-671-7770
www.kerriganart.com
bryan@kerriganart.com

Luminescent Gravel

LUMINESCENT-GRAVEL SAFETY FLOORING

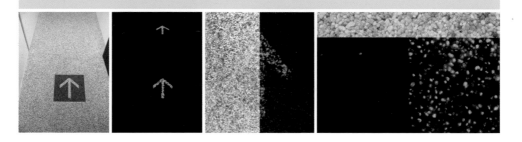

S. Lövenstein BV integrates luminescent particles within gravel floors in order to enhance the emergency-exit signage within a building. The particles can be masked and evenly distributed throughout the surface of the seamless floor, or grouped in patterns like circles, lines, or arrows. They may also be used in combination with various colors of gravel.

In the absence of light, such as in the event of a power outage, the particles become immediately recognizable as an evacuation guidance system. Autonomous, reliable, and maintenance free, Luminescent Gravel thus enhances emergency exiting while mitigating panic.

CONTENTS
Luminescent particles,
gravel

APPLICATIONS
Flooring

TYPES / SIZES
Custom gravel mixture in
various aggregate classes
and colors

ENVIRONMENTAL
Low maintenance

TESTS / EXAMINATIONS
NTA 7909

LIMITATIONS
Application depends on
subsurface structure

CONTACT
S. Lövenstein BV
Hoofdstraat 45
7061 CH Terborg,
Gelderland
The Netherlands
Tel: +31 (0)315 341-967
www.hiddensafety.eu
info@lovenstein.nl

Novec 1230

ZERO OZONE-DEPLETING FIRE-PROTECTION FLUID

3M's Novec 1230 fire-protection fluid is a next-generation halon replacement that balances concerns for human safety, performance, and the environment. Novec 1230 has a zero ozone-depletion potential, an atmospheric lifetime of just five days, and a global warming potential of one.

The fluid can be applied in streaming, total-flooding, inerting, and explosion-suppression applications. It is ideal for special-hazard places where maintaining the operation of high-value equipment is critical. Examples include data-processing and control rooms, telecommunications, marine applications, oil-and-gas applications, strategic military facilities, archives, and museums.

Described as a kind of "dry water," Novec 1230 fluid is stored as a liquid but works as a gas and leaves no messy residue to clean up, allowing systems to remain operational. To demonstrate its effectiveness, 3M has submerged electronic devices in the waterlike substance with no harm to their operations. The nonconductive, noncorrosive, and fast-evaporating fluid is commercially available globally and is suitable for use in occupied spaces.

CONTENTS
Dodecafluoro-2-methylpentan-3-one (CF3CF2C(O)CF(CF3)2)

APPLICATIONS
Fire protection

TYPES / SIZES
2,646 lb (1,200 kg) intermediate bulk containers, 661 lb (300 kg) drums, 11 lb (5 kg) glass sample jugs

ENVIRONMENTAL
Zero ozone-depletion potential, global-warming potential (GWP) of 1, atmospheric lifetime of 5 days

TESTS / EXAMINATIONS
UL2166 Halocarbon Clean Agent Extinguishing Systems Units

LIMITATIONS
Protection of high-value and critical assets

CONTACT
3M
3M Center
Building 224-3N-11
St. Paul, MN 55144
Tel: 800-810-8513
www.3m.com/novec1230fluid

Strong Enviroboard

LOW-EMBODIED-ENERGY FIREPROOF WALLBOARD

Strong Enviroboard (SEB) is a multifunctional wallboard and floorboard composed of magnesium oxide, aerated rock, and recycled cellulose from furniture manufacturing. When layers of ingredients are poured into a mold, the composition bonds exothermically at room temperature, thus requiring no added energy. SEB is made completely of nontoxic materials and cannot grow mold because it is not affected by water.

SEB has virtually no thermal expansion and is immune to freeze-thaw cycles. The combination of SEB with liquid mineral-system coatings offers a 100 percent breathable, fire-, mold-, and waterproof interior or exterior wall without primer. The screw or nail holes come precast, and the board is presanded to smoothness on one side and sanded to be rough on the other for varied surface coatings/attachments. The edges are tapered so that only narrow mud joints are required.

CONTENTS
Magnesium oxide, expanded perlite, recycled-cellulose fiber, glass-fiber mesh

APPLICATIONS
Interior and exterior wall and floor systems

TYPES / SIZES
4' x 7' 7" x 25/64" (1.2 m x 2.3 m x 1 cm), 4' x 7'7" x 1/4" (1.2 m x 2.3 m x 1.8 cm)

ENVIRONMENTAL
No energy consumption, nontoxic, non-mold-harboring, insulating, sound absorbing, produces less dust than standard drywall

TESTS / EXAMINATIONS
ISO 9001:2000, UL Fire Protection Product Certification; other test data available on request

CONTACT
E-Green Building Systems
8421 32nd Avenue SW
Seattle, WA 98126-3703
Tel: 206-219-9236
www.e-greenbuilding systems.clearwire.net
info@e-greenbuilding systems.clearwire.net

Tactile Ceramics

BIOMORPHIC PORCELAIN SCULPTURES

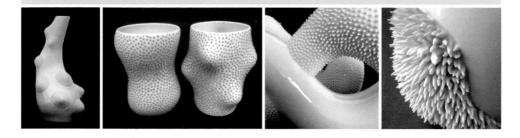

Ikuko Iwamoto's work is influenced by the microscopic world, and she is infatuated with cells, spores, and pollens. Iwamoto's Tactile Ceramics are simultaneously ordinary and extraordinary in nature. They are vehicles to make visible an invisible, microscopic realm. According to the artist, her art conveys a world "of intricacy and detail, of mathematical pattern and organic chaos, of beauty and repulsion." Although her previous conception of porcelain was cool and sharp, she found that porcelain could be rendered to have a smooth and warm quality in order to convey these influences in her sculpture.

CONTENTS
Porcelain

APPLICATIONS
Sculpture, vessels

TYPES / SIZES
3 15/16 to 13 3/4"
(10 to 35 cm)

TESTS / EXAMINATIONS
1000 and 1260°F (537.8
and 682.2°C) firings

LIMITATIONS
Limited edition of 10
to 20 pieces

CONTACT
Ikuko Iwamoto
872 Kobata Shimotsu
Kainan
Wakayama 649-0161
Japan
Tel: +81 (0)73-492-0681
www.ikukoiwamoto.jp
uk@ikukoiwamoto.jp

03: **METAL**

Array

DECORATIVE STEEL SCREEN

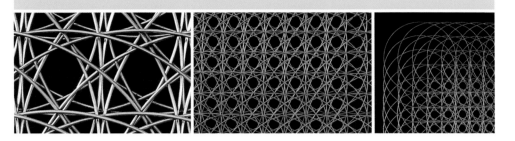

Array is a stainless-steel screen inspired by the decorative economy of patterns in Islamic architecture, mathematical sequences, and growth patterns in nature. It is a product of Sydney-based Korban/Flaubert's focus on the themes of rhythm, sequence, and complexity in design.

Array demonstrates the potential for generating complexity from simple rules: a dense, multi-layered structure arises from a consistent ring size and spacing. Korban/Flaubert's use of ultra-thin stainless steel in such a pattern evokes the delicacy of lacework and other woven textiles—a reference to craft intended to generate tension with the industrial origins of the material itself.

CONTENTS
Welded, electropolished
stainless steel

APPLICATIONS
Spatial divider or sculptural
installation; may be cable
suspended or wall hung

TYPES / SIZES
75 5/8 x 75 5/8"
(192 x 192 cm)

ENVIRONMENTAL
Minimal material use, 100%
recyclable

CONTACT
Korban/Flaubert
8/8-10 Burrows Road
St. Peters
Sydney, NSW 2044
Australia
Tel: +612 9557-6136
www.korbanflaubert
.com.au
info@korbanflaubert
.com.au

ELECTROLESS GOLD-PLATED SCULPTURE

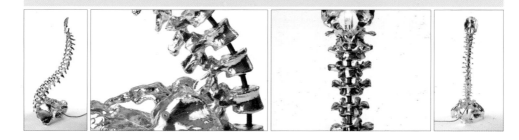

Backlight is a demonstration of electroless metal plating by Tony Wurman of New York–based Wunderwurks. In contrast to conventional electrolytic processes, electroless plating uses a nongalvanic chemical plating method involving multiple reactions in an aqueous solution without external electrical power. Electroless plating can provide decorative and protective finishes for many materials, including metal, wood, glass, plastic, stone, fiberglass, ceramics, and even fabrics.

Wurman's gold-plated light sculpture of a human spine cast in urethane resin demonstrates that the electroless process is highly cost effective compared to conventional electroplating and vacuum metallizing and is not limited to the item's size, design, or surface characteristics. Moreover, the electroless-plated object's finished surface will accept conventional paints to enable striping, accenting with graphics, or airbrushing.

CONTENTS
Urethane, gold plating

APPLICATIONS
Electronics, decorative arts

TYPES / SIZES
Custom

ENVIRONMENTAL
Reduced embodied energy

CONTACT
Coat of Chrome
6390 Sullivan Trail
Wind Gap, PA 18091
Tel: 610-863-1274
www.coatofchrome.com

ULTRAPERFORMING PROCESS

Bloomframe

N° 133413-001

WINDOW FRAME THAT TRANSFORMS INTO A BALCONY

Bloomframe is a window frame that can be transformed into a balcony. Designed by Amsterdam-based Hofman Dujardin Architects, the Bloomframe balcony offers a flexible living environment by making it possible to extend the domain of one's facade. The dynamic balcony can provide additional outdoor space to compact apartments in urban high-rise areas.

The Bloomframe balcony can be operated automatically in one movement and with a single control. The drive consists of an rpm-controlled electric motor that operates the balcony at two points via an auto-braking reduction (drop safety), and the movement is transferred by tie rods from these linear guides. The system includes provisions to guarantee against collapse during opening and closing; the fully open position is limited mechanically, which guarantees optimum safety of the converted balcony. The application of a combined powered and mechanical movement makes the system user-friendly and easy to open and close.

CONTENTS
Insulated-aluminum profiles with steel-reinforced connections, insulated safety glass, sandwich-panel floor, electrical drive with frequency control

APPLICATIONS
Apartments in dense urban areas, hotels, renovations

TYPES / SIZES
Window frame 98 7/16 x 86 5/8" (250 x 220 cm), custom dimensions available

ENVIRONMENTAL
Extension of habitable area, increased light and air

CONTACT
Hofman Dujardin Architects
Haarlemmer Houttuinen 23
1013 GL Amsterdam
The Netherlands
Tel: +31 (0)20 528-64-20
www.hofmandujardin.nl
office@hofmandujardin.nl

ELEVATED AUTOMOBILE STORAGE SYSTEM WITH INTEGRATED DWELLING UNIT

CarLoft is a vehicle storage system devised to reframe the city-dweller's relationship with the automobile. In their development of the technology, CarLoft GmbH set out to recreate the convenience of conventional multiple-level parking structures in dense urban environments.

CarLoft is made possible by CarLift, a vehicle-scaled elevator that transports the car and driver directly from the street to the CarLoggia, or parking space, adjacent to the living unit. CarLoft allows a driver to park quickly (the manufacturer claims two and a half minutes), provides immediate access to the vehicle, and affords the vehicle owner a higher level of security.

CarLoft could be cost effective, eliminating the expense normally required for excavated parking, and provides a structure more attractive than above-grade parking garages or open parking lots. CarLoft may also be used as an extension of a garden, entertaining space, or other storage space (much like the typical suburban driveway) and promises an interesting future for these driveways in the sky.

CONTENTS
CarLift elevator, CarLoggia parking space, aerial garden

APPLICATIONS
Urban multifamily dwelling structures

TYPES / SIZES
Custom

ENVIRONMENTAL
Eliminates environmental impact associated with excavated parking

CONTACT
CarLoft GmbH
Dianastraße 76
13469 Berlin
Germany
Tel: +49 30-434-60-63
www.carloft.com
info@carloft.de

REPURPOSED PRODUCT

City Servings

VESSELS MADE FROM REPURPOSED METALS

City Servings are bowls made from metal washers and discs reclaimed from former industrial uses. Artist Tammy Roy crafts each bowl by hand, welding collections of the flat metal objects together to form graceful, shallow vessels. In her careful repurposing of common industrial materials bound for disposal, Roy demonstrates that recycling can actually be "upcycling," and waste can be made into art.

Roy's Aaben bowl consists of welded metal washers, and the Lukket bowl is made of welded metal discs.

CONTENTS
Reclaimed metal washers
and discs

APPLICATIONS
Container, art object

TYPES / SIZES
Aaben 7 x 3 1/2"
(17.8 x 8.9 cm),
10 x 5 1/2" (25.4 x 14 cm),
13 x 5 1/2" (33 x 14 cm);
Lukket 20 x 3"
(50.8 x 7.6 cm)

ENVIRONMENTAL
Reuse of disposable
material

LIMITATIONS
Indoor use only

CONTACT
Realm Dekor
4308 Timber Valley Drive
Columbus, OH 43230
Tel: 614-893-1089
www.realmdekor.com
info@realmdekor.com

Copper Curtain Wall

COPPER AND COPPER-ALLOY FACADE SYSTEMS

Although copper has been used as a roofing material for centuries, its current application as a curtain-wall material is notable. Copper adds a warmth and richness to building facades just as it does rooftops. Shanghai Kang Yu Jie Sen regards copper as a living material that changes over time depending on environmental factors. In addition to exploiting copper's natural patina, the company also utilizes the malleability of copper to forge three-dimensional shapes and imprint the surface with various images or textures.

CONTENTS
Copper and/or alloy copper with 30% zinc

APPLICATIONS
Exterior and interior facades, roofs, decorative accents

TYPES / SIZES
Maximum size 6' x 5' x 3/16" (1.8 m x 1.5 m x .48 cm), minimum thickness 1/16" (.15 cm)

ENVIRONMENTAL
Easily recycled

CONTACT
Shanghai Kang Yu Jie Sen
Hua-Xiang Road No. 34
Min Hang District
Shanghai 201105
China
Tel: +86 (21) 6-451-8800
www.eastasiaportal.com/luxury
luxury@eastasiaportal.com

EcoSmart Fire

FLUELESS, ENVIRONMENTALLY FRIENDLY FIREPLACES

So deeply embedded is our notion of what a fireplace should be that one's first look at an EcoSmart Fire is typically surprising. The source of fuel is not at all apparent: EcoSmart Fire utilizes denatured ethanol rather than wood, so only the flame is visible. Unlike natural-gas fireplaces, EcoSmart does not require installation or utility connection of a fuel supply.

According to its manufacturer, the Fire Company, EcoSmart Fire makes an efficient and effective heating solution, with an easily regulated flame. EcoSmart installations are defined by minimalist, modern profiles, indicating a refreshing departure from ponderous, traditional masonry boxes. Moreover, their modular construction makes them suitable for most architectural environments.

CONTENTS
Stainless steel

APPLICATIONS
Commercial, residential, and institutional uses

TYPES / SIZES
Burner Kit, Renovator Range, Designer Range, Grate Range, and accessories

ENVIRONMENTAL
Fueled by denatured ethanol, an environmentally friendly and renewable energy

TESTS / EXAMINATIONS
UL Listed, AS4553/AG103

LIMITATIONS
Not suitable for bathrooms or small bedrooms

CONTACT
The Fire Company
9/5 Vuko Place
Warriewood NSW 2102
Australia
Tel: +612 9997-3050
www.ecosmartfire.com
info@ecosmartfire.com

Hanabi

SHAPE-TRANSFORMING LIGHTING FIXTURE

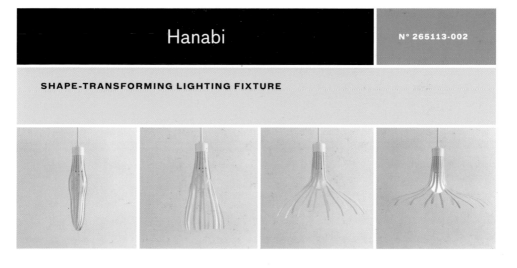

Like the lotus flower, which opens its petals in the presence of the sun and closes them in its absence, Hanabi opens its lamp-shade "petals" when its bulb is turned on and closes them after it has been shut off. Representing an innovative use of shape-memory alloy, the heat of the bulb makes the metal "bloom" whenever the fixture is illuminated. *Hanabi* is the Japanese word for fireworks and literally means "flower fire." Like its namesake, the Hanabi light flickers between beauty and disappearance, embodying the Japanese appreciation of ephemerality.

CONTENTS
Shape memory alloy (SMA), light fixture, cable

APPLICATIONS
Lighting

TYPES / SIZES
10 1/4 x 10 1/4 x 30 11/16"
(26 x 26 x 78 cm)

CONTACT
Nendo Inc.
4-1-20-2A Mejiro
Toshima-ku
Tokyo 171-0031
Japan
Tel: +81 (03) 3954-5554
www.nendo.jp
info@nendo.jp

Hexscreen

HEXAGONAL STEEL SCREEN

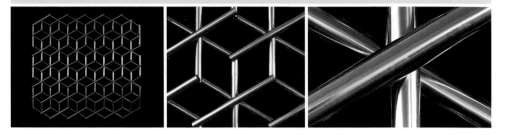

Hexscreen explores the geometry of the hexagon and constructs its simple pattern using repeated identical rods of stainless steel. Inspired by mathematical sequences and natural growth patterns, Hexscreen achieves a visually stimulating effect with a minimum of materials. Hexscreen panels can span from a floor to a ceiling or be wall-mounted. Like Korban/Flaubert's other patterned constructions, it is a product of their focus on rhythm, sequence, and complexity.

CONTENTS
Polished stainless steel

APPLICATIONS
Decorative screen, spatial divider

TYPES / SIZES
78 11/16 x 76 x 3 15/16" (200 x 193 x 10 cm), custom sizes

ENVIRONMENTAL
Efficient use of material, recyclable

CONTACT
Korban/Flaubert
8/8-10 Burrows Road
St. Peters
Sydney NSW 2044
Australia
Tel: +612 9557-6136
www.korbanflaubert
.com.au
info@korbanflaubert
.com.au

PATTERNED CELLULAR GRILL SYSTEMS

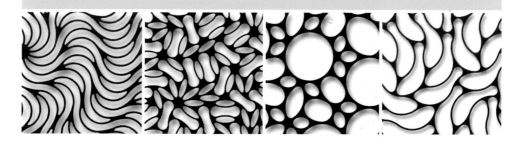

HyperGrill metal tiles are inspired by cellular constructions found in nature. The HyperGrill process approximates the efficiency of cellular compositions in biological surfaces, as well as creating a codified system of patterns that can generate endless tile shapes from a fixed number of sequences. The automated fabrication of these flat, perforated surfaces utilizing lasers or water jets allows for the creation of a variety of repetitive (periodic), nonrepetitive (aperiodic), and random designs that can be customized to different applications.

CONTENTS
Metals or other sheet
materials

APPLICATIONS
Architectural exterior and
interior elements

TYPES / SIZES
Custom

ENVIRONMENTAL
Efficient use of material

CONTACT
Milgo/Bufkin
68 Lombardy Street
Brooklyn, NY 11222
Tel: 718-388-6476
www.milgo-bufkin.com
milgomail@aol.com

InvariMatte

LOW-REFLECTIVITY STAINLESS-STEEL FINISH

InvariMatte is a nondirectional, low-gloss, uniformly textured stainless-steel finish designed for use in architectural applications. While its lower reflectivity lends itself to roofing applications, it can be applied to wall panels, coping, and trim. The superb consistency of this finish results in excellent panel-to-panel matching.

Since InvariMatte has no deteriorating coatings, it can last indefinitely with little maintenance. InvariMatte is readily welded or soldered and is available in coils and cut lengths up to 24 feet (7.3 meters) and widths ranging from 3/4 to 49 inches (1.9 to 124.5 centimeters). Because stainless steel is dimensionally stable up to 2,000°F (1,093°C), InvariMatte provides an added measure of protection in the event of a fire. Contrarian Metal Resources offers a thirty-year warranty on Grades 304, 304L, 316, and 316L.

CONTENTS
Stainless steel

APPLICATIONS
Roofing, wall panels, coping, and trim

TYPES / SIZES
Grades 304, 304L, 316, and 316L; maximum length 24' (7.3 m), width 3/4 to 49" (1.9 to 124.5 cm)

ENVIRONMENTAL
Recycled content, longevity

TESTS / EXAMINATIONS
ASTM A240, A480

CONTACT
Contrarian Metal Resources
20120 Route 19, Suite 207
Cranberry Township, PA
16066
Tel: 724-779-5100
www.metalresources.net
jhalliday@
metalresources.net

VERTICAL-GARDEN WALL SYSTEM

Live Within Skin is a wall system composed of engineered layers of lightweight plant-growth medium. Designed by Greenmeme ecological designer Freya Bardell, the modular vertical garden integrates living vegetation with the built environment so that the walls can be proactively used to address issues of air quality, storm-water runoff, thermal insulation, and sound attenuation.

Live Within Skin walls can serve both interior and exterior applications and may be adapted to most environmental conditions through plant-species selection, integrated irrigation, and lighting. Made up of four main layers consisting of plants, outer surface, growth layers, and irrigation, the modular wall panels may be "pre-grown" or planted on site. Whenever possible, the wall units also incorporate rainwater harvesting and catchment systems. The surfaces are designed with custom screen patterns tailored to the particular plants and growing conditions specified and are fabricated using digitally controlled water-jet or laser-cutting techniques.

CONTENTS
Steel, stone, bioplastics, cladding, felt, coco-coir growing medium, organic-nutrient solution, irrigation

APPLICATIONS
Architectural facades, vertical gardens, fencing and landscape, interior accent walls

TYPES / SIZES
Custom

ENVIRONMENTAL
Native plant material, storm-water retention and management, air filtration, thermal insulation

LIMITATIONS
Each screen is customized to a local environment

CONTACT
Greenmeme
1133 Isabel Street
Los Angeles, CA 90065
Tel: 310-977-8381
www.greenmeme.com
contact.greenmeme@gmail.com

Metal

RECOMBINANT PRODUCT

My Studio

RECYCLABLE OFFICE-FURNITURE SYSTEM

My Studio is an open-plan furniture system that contains 30 percent recycled material and nearly 70 percent recyclable content. Designed by Doug Ball for Herman Miller, My Studio is a human-centered solution featuring design elements that enhance physical and psychological well-being and sense of ownership.

My Studio supports spaces with a reduced footprint and can be utilized for privacy or for collaborative work. The office layout provides capability for creating, displaying, and organizing work. Designed to be a "cubicle without corners," the furniture system has offset connections and rounded corners to give the office a more spacious feel.

CONTENTS
59% steel, 19% wood, 7% aluminum, 6% glass, 4% plastic, 2% laminate, 3% miscellaneous

APPLICATIONS
Workplace furniture

TYPES / SIZES
6 x 6' (1.8 x 1.8 m), 6 x 8' (1.8 x 2.4 m), 8 x 8' (2.4 x 2.4 m), 8 x 10' (2.4 x 3 m), 8 x 12' (2.4 x 3.7 m), 8 x 16' (2.4 x 4.9 m)

ENVIRONMENTAL
69% recyclable, 30% recycled content

TESTS / EXAMINATIONS
GreenGuard Certified

CONTACT
Herman Miller Inc.
855 East Main Avenue
Zeeland, MI 49464
Tel: 888-443-4357
www.hermanmiller.com

PixelSkin02

DYNAMIC SHAPE-MEMORY-ALLOY DISPLAY SYSTEM

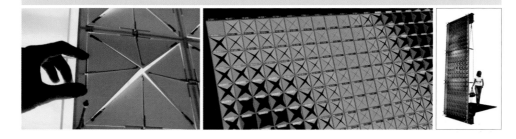

PixelSkin02 explores new possibilities in media-augmented surfaces by employing the mechanical properties inherent in shape memory alloys (SMA). In an attempt to bridge the gap between "lifeless" facade-automation systems and highly expressive yet functionally thin media facades, Orangevoid's Sachin Anshuman developed a matrix of interconnected pixel-tiles that are controlled interactively via embedded electronics.

Described as "electrographic architecture," PixelSkin02 creates a transparent visual field that also generates low-resolution images and low-refresh-rate videos via electromechanical means. Each pixel-tile consists of four triangular panels actuated by 200mA SMA wires. Surface-embedded microcontroller consoles regulate the degree of opening of each panel by adjusting the power supply twenty times per second. Each panel has 255 potential states of adjustment between fully opened or closed, and a technique called "multiplexing" allows for the control of the collection of pixel-tiles in order to create moving patterns and imagery.

CONTENTS
Shape memory alloy (SMA), microcontroller consoles, embedded control electronics, environmental sensors

APPLICATIONS
Dynamic visual-display walls, daylight control, privacy control

TYPES / SIZES
5 7/8 x 5 7/8" (15 x 15 cm) tile

ENVIRONMENTAL
Low-energy consumption

CONTACT
Orangevoid
66 Osbaldeston Road
London N16 7DR
United Kingdom
Tel: +44 (0)20 7502-2239
www.orangevoid.org.uk
info@orangevoid.org.uk

Planium

STAINLESS-STEEL FLOOR SYSTEM

The Gage Planium stainless-steel floor system is a high-tech flooring solution designed for maximum durability and ease of installation. The installation of the patented system eliminates the need for adhesives, cements, or grout. First, a rubber underlayment is installed over any existing level floor. Planium tiles are then aligned to the rubber underlayment and screwed into the integrated blocking plate at the four corners of each tile. The embossed stainless-steel finish was specifically designed to prevent traffic wear.

Planium tiles are only 1/4 inch (.7 centimeters) thick, 23 5/8 x 23 5/8 inches (60 x 60 centimeters), and the reveals are 1/4 inch (.7 centimeters) wide. The rubber underlayment and reveals come in standard black, but custom colors are also available.

CONTENTS
304 stainless-steel veneer,
galvanized-steel core,
rubber underlayment

APPLICATIONS
Flooring

TYPES / SIZES
23 5/8 x 23 5/8 x 1/4"
(60 x 60 x .7 cm), reveals
1/4" (.7 cm)

TESTS / EXAMINATIONS
Reaction to fire—ART
8 Ministerial decree 26/6/84
Class 1; non-slip ASTM-C
1028-89, non-slip DIN S
1130

LIMITATIONS
Not suggested for entry
vestibules

CONTACT
Gage
803 South Black River Street
Sparta, WI 54656
Tel: 866-855-4243
gage@centurytel.net

MODULAR ALUMINUM-PRISM SCREEN SYSTEM

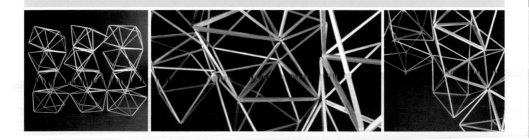

The aggregation of thin, triangular aluminum prisms, which are transformed into intriguing structures that resemble eccentric space-frames, makes up Prism Screen. Inspired by organic growth patterns, Korban/Flaubert developed Prism Screen as a reconfigurable system evoking web formations and branching structures found in nature. Each module consists of twelve interconnected submodules, and the inherent depth of the system creates interesting three-dimensional effects at various viewing angles. Very simple mechanisms can achieve visual complexity based on a systematized logic.

CONTENTS
Aluminum

APPLICATIONS
Decorative screen or sculpture

TYPES / SIZES
94 1/2 x 66 15/16 x 15 3/4"
(240 x 170 x 40 cm),
modular

ENVIRONMENTAL
100% recyclable, minimum
material for maximum effect

CONTACT
Korban/Flaubert
8/8-10 Burrows Road
St. Peters
Sydney NSW 2044
Australia
Tel: +612 9557-6136
www.korbanflaubert
.com.au
info@korbanflaubert
.com.au

MULTIDIMENSIONAL

Sonomorph

SOUND-RESPONSIVE WALL

Inspired by the natural phenomenon of tropism—in which a plant actively responds to external stimuli—designer Natasa Sljivancanin constructed an intelligent kinetic building system that moves in response to changing environmental conditions. A research collaboration with Cornell University, Sljivancanin's sound-responsive wall comprises cellular components that react to various stimuli by opening and closing cells that absorb sound and emit light. Other potential stimuli include light, proximity of people, and touch.

Aluminum outer panels and glass-reinforced plastic inner panels are the components of Sonomorph cells. They are mounted to a simple steel wire net with standard hardware and employ various sensory devices, servo motors, and LED lights for interactive functionality. During the day the cells' polished aluminum shells shimmer in the sunlight, and at night they impart a subtle, colored glow. By involving people in new playful interactions, Sonomorph explores various ways in which augmented physical environments can more extensively and specifically engage their dynamic contexts.

CONTENTS
Aluminum outer panels, glass-reinforced-plastic inner panels, sensory devices, circuit boards, servo motors, wiring, and LED lights

APPLICATIONS
Ecologically sensitive building envelopes, public light infrastructures, storefront display systems, programmable interiors

TYPES / SIZES
12 x 12" (30.5 x 30.5 cm) basic module size; custom dimensions possible

ENVIRONMENTAL
Biomimetic system

CONTACT
Natasa Sljivancanin
Waldermarshage 6
0175 Oslo
Norway
Tel: 479-302-6089
www.biomaterialism.com
info@biomaterialism.com

Steel Tongue

WOVEN ALUMINUM AND STEEL CHAIR

Steel Tongue chair is inspired by the pierced tongue. The Project Import Export design is hand-crafted with stainless-steel wire and recyclable aluminum strips. Adapting cradle-to-cradle concepts, Steel Tongue's aluminum strips are easily disassembled and reusable on another chair with another shape. This process requires a minimal amount of energy and resource consumption.

CONTENTS
Stainless-steel frame,
recyclable aluminum strips

APPLICATIONS
Seating, sculpture

TYPES / SIZES
20 x 31 x 24" (50 x 80 x 60 cm)

ENVIRONMENTAL
Recyclable aluminum strips,
design for disassembly,
low-energy manufacturing

LIMITATIONS
Indoor and covered outdoor
lounge chair

CONTACT
Project Import Export
19331 Southwest 31st Court
Miramar, FL 33029
Tel: 786-543-3037
www.projectimportexport
.com
info@projectimportexport
.com

xGnP

EXFOLIATED GRAPHITE NANO-PLATELETS

Exfoliated Graphite Nano-Platelets (xGnP) is a new type of nanoparticle made from graphite. These nanoparticles consist of small stacks of graphene that are 1 to 15 nanometers thick, with diameters ranging from sub-micron to 100 microns. Since xGnP is composed of the same material as carbon nanotubes, it shares many of their electrochemical characteristics, although not their tensile strength. The platelet shape, however, offers xGnP edges that are easier to modify chemically for enhanced dispersion in polymers.

Composite materials made with polymers, like plastics, nylon, or rubber, can be made electrically or thermally conductive with the addition of small amounts of xGnP. These nanoparticles can change the fundamental properties of plastics, enabling them to perform more like metals with metallic properties. These new nanoparticles also improve barrier properties, modulus, and surface toughness when used in composites.

CONTENTS
Graphite

APPLICATIONS
Advanced composite materials, thermally and electrically conductive polymers

TYPES / SIZES
Particle diameters ranging from submicron to 15+ microns

LIMITATIONS
Base compositions of graphite are colored black

CONTACT
XG Sciences Inc.
5020 Northwind Drive,
Suite 212
East Lansing, MI 48823
Tel: 517-203-1110
www.xgsciences.com
m.knox@xgsciences.com

04: **WOOD**

Accoya

ACETYLATED WOOD

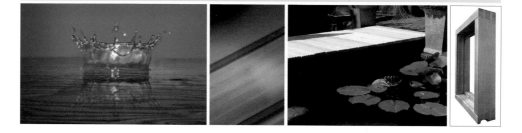

Accoya is a high-performance solid wood that is modified by a proprietary process called acetylization. This technique increases the amount of acetyl molecules, which are naturally present in all species of wood, throughout the material (not just at the surface). Acetylization delivers exceptional performance attributes, including Class 1 durability, reduced swelling and shrinkage, mold and insect resistance, UV-degradation resistance, and reduced thermal conductivity. Because of these factors, Accoya is appropriate for use in more rigorous conditions, such as heavy-traffic road bridges. The product is also sourced from sustainable forests, is 100 percent recyclable, and is nontoxic.

CONTENTS
100% wood

APPLICATIONS
Exterior and interior wood framing, siding, cladding, decking, doors, trim, furniture

TYPES / SIZES
Various, with a maximum thickness of 3 15/16" (10 cm) from solid wood

ENVIRONMENTAL
100% recyclable, sourced from sustainably managed forests, nontoxic

TESTS / EXAMINATIONS
Test results available on request

LIMITATIONS
Not suitable for saltwater marine application, not termite resistant

CONTACT
Titan Wood Limited
Kensington Centre
66 Hammersmith Road
London W14 8UD
United Kingdom
Tel: +44 (0)20-8114-2510
www.accoya.info
info@accoya.info

WALL-MOUNTED SHELVING SYSTEM

Designers Johannes Herbertsson and Karl-Henrik Rennstam created the Alog shelf based on the wall-hung magazine rack. Noting that the longevity of a magazine issue varies according to a subscriber's interest in its content, Herbertsson and Rennstam designed a shelving system to allow for the easy rearrangement and alteration of shelves in relation to the ongoing flow of small and large, thick and thin magazines in a typical library.

Alog consists of removable shelves that are inserted into a wall-mounted panel with a grooved surface. The shelves are locked into place by their own weight, thus eliminating the need for any extra fittings.

CONTENTS
Medium-density fiberboard (MDF), ash

APPLICATIONS
Shelving

TYPES / SIZES
25 1/2 x 25 1/2 x 1"
(64.8 x 64.8 x 2.5 cm)

ENVIRONMENTAL
Backing panel 99% postindustrial recycled material

LIMITATIONS
Not for exterior use

CONTACT
VUJJ
Mäster Nilsgatan 1
211-26 Malmö
Sweden
Tel: +46 40-972760
www.vujj.com
info@vujj.com

Clamp-a-leg

SET OF LEGS TO MAKE AN INSTANT TABLE

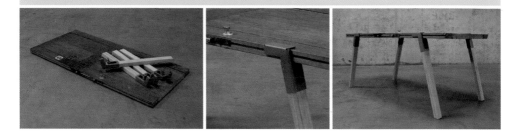

Jorre van Ast's Clamp-a-leg is designed to transform old planar surfaces into new table tops with minimal materials. The set of four wood-and-cast-metal legs represents a more compact alternative to trestles and may be used in conjunction with a door, panel, or other flat surface of adequate thickness to create a new horizontal surface with nominal installation time.

CONTENTS
Wood, cast metal

APPLICATIONS
Tables, desks, counters

TYPES / SIZES
7 7/8 x 29 1/2 x 2 3/8"
(20 x 75 x 6 cm)

ENVIRONMENTAL
Reuse of old surfaces

CONTACT
Jorre van Ast
35 Bentley Road
London N1 4BY
United Kingdom
Tel: +44 (0)20-8880-0690
www.jorrevanast.com
info@jorrevanast.com

END-GRAIN COCONUT-PALM SOLID SURFACING

CocoBlock is a solid surface material made entirely of coconut palm that has been specially engineered to reveal its naturally fibrous end grain within a geometric pattern of bonded strips. Developed for horizontal surfacing applications by Smith and Fong, this material is available as an unfinished slab and is ideal for both commercial and residential table tops, reception counters, and bar tops. It can be stained or used in its natural mahoganylike color.

CocoBlock must be sealed on all sides with food-grade tongue oil, conversion varnish, or some other environmentally preferable sealant. Smith and Fong uses only 100 percent reclaimed coconut palm for all its palm oil-based products, and no formaldehyde or toxic substances are added.

CONTENTS
Coconut palm

APPLICATIONS
Horizontal commercial and residential applications

TYPES / SIZES
30 x 72 x 1 1/2"
(76.2 x 182.9 x 3.8 cm)

ENVIRONMENTAL
100% reclaimed material; no added formaldehyde or other toxins

LIMITATIONS
Not recommended for vertical applications; must be fully supported and sealed on all sides

CONTACT
Robin Reigi Inc.
48 West 21st Street
New York, NY 10010
Tel: 212-924-5558
www.robin-reigi.com
info@robin-reigi.com

Ecotextures

ARCHITECTURAL PANELS CRAFTED FROM ENVIRONMENTALLY FRIENDLY OSB

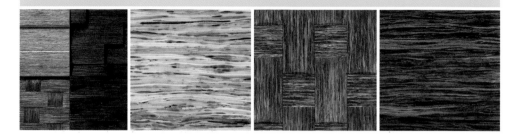

Rapidly renewable timber is used to create Architectural Systems' Ecotextures, architectural panels crafted from environmentally friendly oriented strand board (OSB). Durable and shrink resistant, Ecotextures panels have a distinctive grain and are appropriate for millwork, feature walls, column covers, fixtures, and furniture. No urea-formaldehydes are used, and component lumber is Sustainable Forestry Initiative (SFI) certified.

Panel sizes vary to facilitate easy installation and include Tiers, Basketweave, and Pyramids planks as well as Stripes interlocking bars. Coordinating 4 x 8 foot (1.2 x 2.4 meter) flat-panel-sheet goods are available, and factory color finishes and fire rating are also available for all patterns.

CONTENTS
Oriented strand board
(OSB)

APPLICATIONS
Wall panels, coordinated
flat panels for walls and
flooring

TYPES / SIZES
Tiers 9 3/4 x 90" (24.8 x
228.6 cm), Basketweave
9 5/8 x 92 3/8" (24.4 x 234.7
cm), Pyramids 10 1/2 x 88"
(26.7 x 223.5 cm), Stripes
4 x 96" (10.2 x 243.8 cm) or
8 x 96" (20.3 x 243.8 cm)

ENVIRONMENTAL
Sustainable Forestry
Initiative (SFI) certified

CONTACT
Architectural Systems Inc.
150 West 25th Street
8th Floor
New York, NY 10001
Tel: 212-206-1730
www.archsystems.com
sales@archsystems.com

WOOD MOSAIC TILES

Fortis Arbor wood mosaics are made by shaping and finishing exotic hardwoods made from plantation-grown lumber. The tiles are handcrafted from solid bamboo, teak, and rosewood. These woods were selected because they exhibit superior strength and durability as well as an appealing color range.

To make their products, Flux Studios partnered with a small furniture company in order to reclaim wood from plantation-grown lumber too small to be used for furniture. Unlike homogeneous ceramic tiles, Fortis Arbor tiles express the diverse patterns and coloration naturally present in the wood and bamboo materials used. Since each tile is cut and finished by hand, each installation is unique.

Fortis Arbor mosaics can be used in virtually any interior application with limited water exposure: on walls, countertops, backsplashes, fireplace surrounds, and high-traffic floors in kitchens and bathrooms. Installation of the tiles requires Fortis Arbor grout, developed for the particular expansion and contraction characteristics of the wood.

CONTENTS
Plantation-grown wood and bamboo

APPLICATIONS
Floors, walls, countertops, backsplashes

TYPES / SIZES
1 x 1 x 1/4" (2.5 x 2.5 x .6 cm) and 1 x 2 x 1/4" (2.5 x 5.1 x .6 cm)

ENVIRONMENTAL
Sustainably harvested and plantation-grown wood reclaimed from furniture making

LIMITATIONS
Not for exterior use, not for wet applications, must be installed with proprietary grouting system

CONTACT
Flux Studios Inc.
4001 North Ravenswood Avenue, #603
Chicago, IL 60613
Tel: 773-883-2030
www.fluxstudios.com
fluxstudios@sbcglobal.net

Husque

MACADAMIA-NUT-SHELL COMPOSITE

Before 1857, the macadamia nut grew nowhere else except on the mid–east coast of Australia. Australia is the largest producer of the macadamia and generates a large amount of discarded shells.

Queensland-based designer Marc Harrison seized this opportunity to reuse this waste material to create beautiful new products. After the macadamia kernels are removed, Harrison mills the discarded shells into fine particles and melds them with a polymer. He then molds the composite into various functional objects and surfaces.

Not dissimilar in appearance to Bakelite, Husque has a silky texture that can be enhanced by polishing with macadamia oil or wax timber polishes. It can be machined and has extensive applications in design and architecture. Husque can be lined with colors that can be machine polished to lacquerlike mirror finishes.

CONTENTS
Macadamia nut shell,
polymer

APPLICATIONS
Vessels, trays, containers

TYPES / SIZES
Custom

ENVIRONMENTAL
Recycled byproduct of the
macadamia-nut industry

LIMITATIONS
Bleaching may occur with
exterior use

CONTACT
Husque Pty Ltd.
PO Box 210
Moorooka, Queensland
4105
Australia
Tel: + 61 (0)43-944-2928
www.husque.com
info@husque.com

Iconic Panels

CARVED MDF RELIEF PANELS WITH A FORMED LAMINATE SURFACE

One of the major outcomes of computer-driven fabrication technology is a renewed interest in ornament and pattern making. Products like Iconic Panels, which are carved relief panels that are typically seen at room-encompassing scales, are part ornament, part environmental graphics, and part basic building blocks.

Developed by B&N Industries, Iconic Panels consist of formed laminate over a carved medium-density fiberboard (MDF) core in a variety of patterns. The panels can be sawn, nailed, screwed, glued, or simply mounted on walls with special panel cleats. Iconic Panels are available in eleven patterns and eleven colors and can be outfitted with a variety of manufacturer-provided shelving and accessory hardware.

CONTENTS
Medium-density fiberboard
(MDF), laminate

APPLICATIONS
Walls

TYPES / SIZES
11 sizes and 11 colors,
46 x 96" (116.8 x 243.8 cm)

ENVIRONMENTAL
May be ordered with a
no-formaldehyde-added
MDF comprised of 100%
recovered and recycled
wood fibers

TESTS / EXAMINATIONS
Fire Rating I panels
available

LIMITATIONS
Interior use only

CONTACT
B&N Industries
1409 Chapin Avenue
Burlingame, CA 94010
Tel: 650-593-4127
www.bnind.com
jshader@bnind.com

Leech

WOVEN LIANA CHAISE

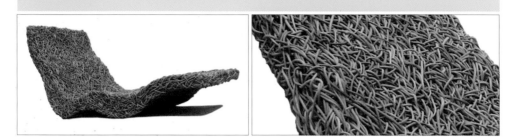

Liana is a category of climbing vines found in tropical and temperate forests. In some forests, overgrown liana can create congestion and is often cut down and destroyed. Liana species such as rattan are rapidly renewable plants that may be harvested several times a year.

Designed by Project Import Export, the Leech chaise combines a woven-liana skin and thin, welded steel wire. In this intriguing combination, liana provides strength and durability while the steel provides a shapable framework. Like other Project Import Export products, Leech is fabricated using nontoxic additives as well as low energy-consumption and pollution-free practices.

CONTENTS
Woven-liana skin, steel frame

APPLICATIONS
Seating

TYPES / SIZES
24 x 65 x 30"
(60 x 140 x 80 cm)

ENVIRONMENTAL
Rapidly renewable material

LIMITATIONS
Requires covering for exterior use (dry climates only)

CONTACT
Project Import Export
19331 Southwest 31st Court
Miramar, FL 33029
Tel: 786-543-3037
www.projectimport
export.com
info@projectimport
export.com

Maplex

SUPERIOR PERFORMANCE MEDIUM- AND HIGH-DENSITY FIBERBOARD

Maplex is an environmentally responsible alternative to traditional wood building materials. Maplex P (Performance) is a high-density fiberboard with twice the bending and tensile strengths of birch plywood of the same thickness. Maplex C (Contour) is a medium-density board, ideal for forming and bending into smooth curves. Both types of Maplex can be machined, bent, rolled, formed, punched, and laminated, as well as stained, painted, printed, dyed, and coated with a wide variety of finishing products.

Maplex is made of thin plies of softwood tree fibers. These fibers undergo a unique process that increases their surface area, boosting their potential for hydrogen bonding. Heat and pressure are then applied, releasing moisture and creating a strong, pliable fiber matrix. Maplex is manufactured without the use of bleach, binders, formaldehyde, petroleum-based products, or other off-gassing chemicals. Because no resins are used, the formability and appearance of Maplex is superior to other fiberboard products.

CONTENTS
100% unbleached wood fiber

APPLICATIONS
Wall surfacing, furniture, exhibits, displays, signage

TYPES / SIZES
Maplex P (Performance) and Maplex C (Contour); sheet thickness 1/16, 1/8, 3/16, 1/4, and 5/16" (.15, .32, .48, .6, and .8 cm); sheet sizes 4 x 8' (1.2 x 2.4 m), 5'3" x 10'2" (1.6 x 3.1 m), 6'3" x 10'10" (1.9 x 3.3 m); custom sheet sizes available

ENVIRONMENTAL
100% recyclable and biodegradable, made from a renewable resource, no chemicals or additives used in the manufacturing process, low VOCs

TESTS / EXAMINATIONS
ASTM D-3394, D-202, D-695, D-790, D-732

LIMITATIONS
Not recommended for exterior use

CONTACT
Weidmann
1 Gordon Mills Way
St. Johnsbury, VT 05819
Tel: 802-748-8106
www.maplexmaterial.com
info@maplexmaterial.com

Plyboo Neapolitan

SHREDDED AND COMPRESSED BAMBOO OVER SOLID BAMBOO SUBSTRATE

Made from bamboo-strand technology, Smith and Fong's Plyboo Neapolitan is a durable, stable, and sustainable alternative to exotic hardwoods like zebrawood and ebony. Made from light and dark strands of shredded bamboo with a non-urea formaldehyde adhesive over multiple plies of cross-laminated bamboo, Neapolitan panels are extremely dense and stable.

Suitable for nearly any surface or plywood application, Plyboo Neapolitan is sold presanded and unfinished as a panel, and prefinished or unfinished as flooring. The product may be stained or clear coated and does not require edge banding. The Neapolitan striped pattern is rendered randomly during fabrication.

CONTENTS
Bamboo, resin

APPLICATIONS
Millwork, doors, walls,
furniture, flooring

TYPES / SIZES
30 x 72 x 3/4"
(76.2 x 182.9 x 1.9 cm)

ENVIRONMENTAL
Substitute for less-
sustainable hardwoods, low
VOCs

TESTS / EXAMINATIONS
Can be made with a Class
A fire rating

LIMITATIONS
Not for exterior use

CONTACT
Robin Reigi Inc.
48 West 21st Street
New York, NY 10010
Tel: 212-924-5558
www.robin-reigi.com
info@robin-reigi.com

FORM-PRESSED VENEER PANELS

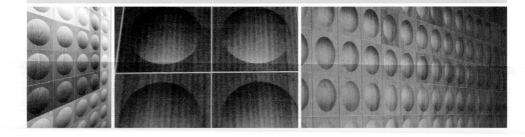

POP is a form-pressed-plywood panel system featuring three-dimensional convex impressions in a variety of wood and other finishes. POP is manufactured in Finland in two sizes: 7 7/8 x 7 7/8 inches (20 x 20 centimeters) and 15 3/4 x 15 3/4 inches (40 x 40 centimeters). Wood-finish options include birch, cherry, walnut, and wenge, and these finishes are laminated with invisible matte film to facilitate cleaning. White lacquer, black lacquer, and sound-absorbing cork finishes are also available. POP panels are mounted with concealed aluminum fittings for a clean aesthetic effect.

CONTENTS
Pressed plywood, wood-veneer, or cork surface

APPLICATIONS
Walls and ceilings

TYPES / SIZES
15 3/4 x 15 3/4" (40 x 40 cm),
7 7/8 x 7 7/8" (20 x 20 cm)

ENVIRONMENTAL
Wood veneers are sourced
from certified sustainable
forests

CONTACT
Hightower Group
200 Lexington Avenue
Studio 1316
New York, NY 10016
Tel: 212-725-3509
www.hightoweraccess.com
service@hightoweraccess
.com

MULTIDIMENSIONAL PRODUCT

Riddled

PERFORATED WOOD AND ALUMINUM STORAGE CUPBOARD

Riddled represents the latest phase of Steven Holl's explorations of cellular geometries and perforated surfaces. Designed by Holl with Nick Gelpi, Riddled consists of five wood-paneled compartments, each perforated with a different variety of pattern. Constructed with laser-cutting processes, these modules are made from flat sheets with door openings without metal hinges. The compartments fit together with aluminum infill panels to create a complete, structurally stable unit.

CONTENTS
Walnut-veneer panels,
anodized aluminum

APPLICATIONS
Storage, sculptural
installation

TYPES / SIZES
8 3/4 x 19 11/16 x 27 9/16"
(200 x 50 x 70 cm), 28 3/4 x
19 11/16 x 79 15/16"
(73 x 50 x 203 cm); 5/64"
(.2 cm) walnut veneer with
vegetable oil finish

ENVIRONMENTAL
Recyclable

TESTS / EXAMINATIONS
Passed CATAS tests for
50,000 openings

LIMITATIONS
Not for exterior use

CONTACT
Horm srl
Via San Giuseppe, 25
33082 Azzano Decimo
Italy
Tel: +39 (0)434-640733
www.horm.it
horm@horm.it

MULTILAYERED POLYCHROMATIC WOOD BENCH

In Ripples, Toyo Ito draws his inspiration from the movement of concentric circles formed when a pebble is thrown into the water. The profiles of Ito's wood seats are reminiscent of anatomical shapes of people of varying statures—men and women, robust and skinny, old and young. One-quarter-inch (.6 cm) thick layers in varying colors and types of solid wood are processed on a pantograph to create a polychromatic effect. Horm manufactured Ripples in ninety-nine numbered models, each signed by Ito.

CONTENTS
Multilayered solid natural wood of different types and colors

APPLICATIONS
Seating, sculpture

TYPES / SIZES
78 3/4 x 19 11/16 x 15 3/4"
(200 x 50 x 40 cm)

ENVIRONMENTAL
Recyclable

LIMITATIONS
Only 99 models produced

CONTACT
Horm srl
Via San Giuseppe, 25
33082 Azzano Decimo
Italy
Tel: +39 (0)434-640733
www.horm.it
horm@horm.it

Sendai

GLASS SHELVING WITH CONICAL WOOD SUPPORTS

Toyo Ito's Sendai shelf sculpture is highly reminiscent of his architectural tour de force by the same name. Like the Sendai Mediatheque, the structural elements of the shelf are comprised of conical sections of varying diameters, rising up through glass planes like abstracted bamboo or seaweed. Unlike the Mediatheque, however, these vertical elements are solid, slender trunks of various types of wood. The wood planes that are laminated and sculpted into conical forms are all oriented vertically, lending a strong vertical grain and eerie lightness to the work. The glass is printed, drilled, sanded, painted, and tempered.

CONTENTS
60 trunks of conic plywood (each one different from the next), 6 sanded glass shelves

APPLICATIONS
Display, storage, sculpture

TYPES / SIZES
86 5/8 x 15 x 76 3/8" (220 x 38 x 194 cm)

ENVIRONMENTAL
Recyclable

CONTACT
Horm srl
Via San Giuseppe, 25
33082 Azzano Decimo
Italy
Tel: +39 (0)434-640733
www.horm.it
horm@horm.it

WOVEN-RATTAN LOUNGE CHAIR

Designed and fabricated by Project Import Export, Space Hog is inspired by the human womb and is intended to be viewed from the rear of the chair, where a small opening symbolizes the birth canal. The woven-rattan patterns signify the texture and consistency of the venous configuration of the womb. Rattan is a plant that can be harvested several times a year. Space Hog is made using non-polluting, low-energy processes without the use of toxic additives.

CONTENTS
Rattan frame and woven
rattan skin

APPLICATIONS
Seating

TYPES / SIZES
4 x 5 x 6' (1.2 x 1.5 x 1.8 m)

ENVIRONMENTAL
Rapidly renewable
materials

LIMITATIONS
Must be covered for
exterior use

CONTACT
Project Import Export
19331 Southwest 31st Court
Miramar, FL 33029
Tel: 786-543-3037
www.projectimportexport
.com
info@projectimportexport
.com

Tambour

BAMBOO AND COCONUT-PALM STRIPS WITH A CLOTH BACKING

Smith and Fong's Tambour is a flexible, lightweight panel that is a cost effective and highly durable solution for curved and flat walls, doors, column surrounds, ceiling panels, and furniture components. Tambour is made from individual strips of finished, unfinished, and raw bamboo strips in 4 x 8 foot (1.2 x 2.4 meter) panels or unfinished and finished coconut palm in 2 1/2 x 6 foot (.8 x 1.8 meter) panels. The material may be cut with typical woodworking tools and preferably applied with a low-VOC adhesive.

CONTENTS
Bamboo or coconut palm,
fabric backing

APPLICATIONS
Vertical panels, cabinetry
facing, doors, ceiling
panels, column covers,
furniture

TYPES / SIZES
4 x 8' (1.2 x 2.4 m) or
2'–6" x 6' (.8 x 1.8 m)

ENVIRONMENTAL
Rapidly renewable

LIMITATIONS
Not recommended for
flooring

CONTACT
Robin Reigi Inc.
48 West 21st Street
New York, NY 10010
Tel: 212-924-5558
www.robin-reigi.com
info@robin-reigi.com

WOVEN WATER-HYACINTH DAYBED

According to the University of Florida Center for Aquatic Plants, water hyacinth is one of the most invasive plants. Water hyacinth was introduced to Florida from South America in the 1880s and has grown profusely since, covering up to 125,000 acres of water. Water hyacinth populations can double in twelve days, and infestations crowd out native plants, reduce fisheries, and weaken biological diversity.

In order to protect local habitats, water-hyacinth plants are cut down. Designer Bannavis Sribyatta collects the waste material from these menacing plants and give them a new life in the form of the Tonecoon daybed. Inspired by the flower petals of Tonecoon trees grown in Thailand and several other parts of Asia, the daybed is constructed of woven water-hyacinth fiber wrapped around a rattan frame. It is completely handcrafted using nonpolluting, low-energy processes, and the rattan comes from rapidly renewable sources.

CONTENTS
Water-hyacinth fiber, rattan frame

APPLICATIONS
Seating

TYPES / SIZES
6'6" x 6'6" x 3'
(2 x 2 x .9 m)

ENVIRONMENTAL
Utilizes invasive-plant waste, rapidly renewable materials

LIMITATIONS
Outdoor use requires cover

CONTACT
Project Import Export
19331 Southwest 31st Court
Miramar, FL 33029
Tel: 786-543-3037
www.projectimport
export.com
info@projectimport
export.com

Tropical Veneer Collection

RAPIDLY RENEWABLE VENEER PANELS FROM SOUTH AMERICA

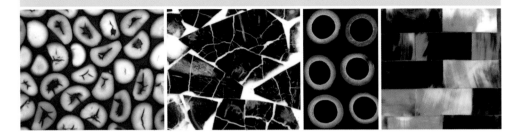

Tropical Veneer Collection consists of handcrafted veneer materials from South America, featuring rapidly renewable and commonly occurring materials, such as coconut and totumo shell, plantain bark, tagua seed, and pearlstone. These products are combined with medium-density fiberboard (MDF) and resins to create stable panels. Different colored resins can be used to contribute additional dimensions and colors, and several materials can be used in combination to produce striking designs for wall applications, doors, furniture, and decorative elements.

CONTENTS
Medium-density fiberboard (MDF), resin, various natural materials

APPLICATIONS
Wall panels, table surfaces

TYPES / SIZES
2 x 4' (.6 x 1.2 m) panels; additional dimensions and shapes available

ENVIRONMENTAL
Rapidly renewable materials

CONTACT
Architectural Systems Inc.
150 West 25th Street
8th Floor
New York, NY 10001
Tel: 212-206-1730
www.archsystems.com
sales@archsystems.com

WoodSure

ACRYLIC-INFUSED WOOD

WoodSure is natural wood that has been infused with acrylic resin, which enhances both the beauty of the wood and its durability. The acrylic-infused process converts wood into a dimensionally stable material that repels water, resists dents and abrasions, and is much harder than untreated wood. This process allows abundant softwoods to be used in the place of scarcer hardwoods. WoodSure's proprietary acrylic-infused process also intensifies the wood-grain pattern, amplifying the drama of wood's natural internal structure.

CONTENTS
Wood, acrylic

APPLICATIONS
Flooring, countertops, furniture, paneling, moldings, doors, frames, tools

TYPES / SIZES
Standard lumber sizes

ENVIRONMENTAL
Improves durability of wood, allows abundant softwoods to replace hardwoods

LIMITATIONS
50% heavier than untreated wood

CONTACT
WoodSure
2475 Progress Way
P.O. Box 299
Woodburn, OR 97071
Tel: 1-800-770-7523
www.woodsure.com
jsouthwell@woodsure.com

Wovin Wall

MULTIDIMENSIONAL WALL AND CEILING PANEL SYSTEM

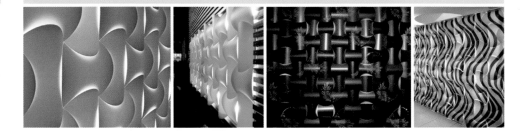

The Wovin Wall is a simple, modular panel system that utilizes depth for dramatic effect. It consists of tiles supported on a lightweight mounting grid, which can be fixed to any wall or ceiling surface, light box, or display. Wovin tiles are available in many finishes, including wood, laminate, polypropylene, and metal, and are clipped into the supporting grid in alternating directions to create a distinctive, seamless woven pattern. The tiles are offered in two standard sizes and may be printed with tiled digital images to create a large, undulating image field. Translucent tiles may be backlit with standard fluorescent lights, and these tiles can be effective in ceiling-retrofit applications beneath existing light fixtures.

CONTENTS
Aluminum frame, wood, laminate, polypropylene, or anodized aluminum tiles

APPLICATIONS
Feature walls and ceilings, immersive graphics, light-box displays

TYPES / SIZES
Standard, oval

ENVIRONMENTAL
Rapidly renewable or recycled content

TESTS / EXAMINATIONS
Available upon request

LIMITATIONS
Not for exterior use

CONTACT
Wovin Wall
6-8 Ricketty Street, Mascot
Sydney NSW 2020
Australia
Tel: 612-9317-0222
www.wovinwall.com
esales@wovinwall.com

05: PLASTIC + RUBBER

100 Percent

COMPRESSED 100% POSTCONSUMER RECYCLED HDPE

100 Percent is a material designed to have a minimal environmental footprint. Made entirely from postconsumer recycled high-density polyethylene (HDPE), it is waste transformed into engineered panels for design applications. 100 Percent is derived from recycled household packaging materials, such as milk and detergent bottles. Recent advances in sorting and cleaning technologies are used to recapture waste materials, which are first organized by color and then recombined into a variety of designs via a compression process.

Recycled HDPE panels are UV stable and ideally suited for education, science, and healthcare environments. Superior chemical-resistance properties also make these panels appropriate for applications like work surfaces and restroom partitions. The collection includes compressed particles of carefully chosen colors in neutral tones with chromatic accents.

CONTENTS
100% postconsumer recycled high-density polyethylene

APPLICATIONS
Doors, work surfaces, restroom partitions, decking materials, trim molding

TYPES / SIZES
Tumbled finish 4'7" x 10' (1.4 x 3.0 m); polished finish 4' x 10' (1.2 x 3.0 m); gauge: 1" (2.5 cm)

ENVIRONMENTAL
100% postconsumer recycled content

LIMITATIONS
Maximum temperature use not to be above 150°F (65.6°C)

CONTACT
3form
2300 West 2300 South
Salt Lake City, UT 84119
Tel: 800-726-0126
www.3-form.com
info@3-form.com

Abacá

HIGH-PRESSURE LAMINATE WITH RECYCLED BANANA FIBERS

Named for a species of banana harvested primarily for use as fiber in the production of rope and twine, Abacá employs residues from banana harvesting and recycles them into a high-pressure decorative laminate with 40 percent postindustrial recovered content. The fibers are sprinkled over an array of background colors to yield a random, nondirectional design and texture.

Abacá is offered in ten natural hues in 4 x 10 foot (1.2 x 3 meter) sheets, with a standard grade thickness of 6/125 inches (.12 centimeters). Abacá is suitable for both horizontal and vertical applications where high-impact resistance and durability are required.

CONTENTS
Phenolic resin-impregnated kraft sheets, decorative paper, recycled banana fibers

APPLICATIONS
Horizontal and vertical interior surfaces

TYPES / SIZES
4 x 10' (1.2 x 3 m) sheets, 6/125" (.12 cm) thick

ENVIRONMENTAL
Recycled banana plant fibers (1% of total product weight)

TESTS / EXAMINATIONS
NEMA Pub LD3-2005, Section 2

LIMITATIONS
Not for exterior use; not recommended for direct application to plaster, gypsum wallboard, or concrete

CONTACT
Lamin-Art
1670 Basswood Road
Schaumburg, IL 60173
Tel: 800-323-7624
www.laminart.com
info@laminart.com

Accura Bluestone

ENGINEERED NANOCOMPOSITE FOR STEREOLITHOGRAPHY

3D Systems' stereolithography process creates three-dimensional objects using a laser to cure sequential layers of material to form shapes that have been modeled in digital environments. Accura Bluestone is an engineered nanocomposite designed specifically for this process.

Accura Bluestone is an exceptionally rigid, thermally resistant material, making it suitable for scaled automotive and aerospace wind-tunnel applications. Bluestone has also been used in the design verification of lighting components, as well as the production of jigs and fixtures for complex assembly operations.

CONTENTS
Nanocomposite epoxy resin

APPLICATIONS
Prototyping, modeling, testing, jig fabrication

TYPES / SIZES
Custom

ENVIRONMENTAL
No material waste

LIMITATIONS
Limited durability

CONTACT
3D Systems Corporation
333 Three D Systems Circle
Rock Hill, SC 29730
Tel: 803-326-4080
www.3dsystems.com
moreinfo@3dsystems.com

FIRE-RESISTANT HONEYCOMB COMPOSITE PANEL

Design Composite's unique bonding technology enables the combination of a rigid, translucent honeycomb core with transparent thermoplastic top sheets, resulting in a panel with exceptional optical features.

AIR-board's common properties include excellent light transmission, outstanding thermal insulation, high stiffness, and light weight. The composite panel is compatible with standard profile systems and is easy to handle and process. The polycarbonate honeycomb core is also nonflammable. The six types of AIR-boards differ in top sheet material and structure, dimensions, and colors.

CONTENTS
Polycarbonate, acrylic

APPLICATIONS
Interior and exterior applications, shop fitting, exhibitions and events

TYPES / SIZES
AIR-board PC, UV PC, UV PC color, UV satin, color UV PC, metal UV PC; 100 3/8 x 41 5/16" x 15/32 / 5/8 / 3/4" (255 x 105 x 1.2/1.6/1.9 cm),118 7/8 x 48 x 3/4" (302 x 122 x 1.9 cm), or 118 7/8 x 39 3/8 x 3/4" (302 x 100 x 1.9 cm); panel sizes: 307 x 79 1/2 x 5 7/8" (780 x 202 x 15 cm) maximum size

ENVIRONMENTAL
100% recyclable

TESTS / EXAMINATIONS
Fire class B1–DIN 4102, B1-ÖNORM B 3800, 1Y-BS476 Part 7

LIMITATIONS
Not thermoformable, flat applications only

CONTACT
Design Composite GmbH
Klausgasse 32
5730 Mittersill, Salzburg
Austria
Tel: +43-6562-40609-0
www.design-composite
.com
info@design-composite
.com

Alabaster

STYRENE-BASED UNSATURATED RESIN

A rich incandescence emanates from 3form's new warm, translucent product made of styrene-based unsaturated resin. Drawing the creamy colors and swirls of pure gypsum into a more malleable polyresin panel, Alabaster becomes a material alternative for everything from lighting panels to furnishings and privacy panels. This new polymeric resin sheet is chemically resistant, possesses excellent rigidity, is lightweight, and has a renewable surface that extends the product life and aesthetic appeal.

CONTENTS

Styrene-based unsaturated resin, calcium carbonate, silicone

APPLICATIONS

Countertops, backsplashes, wall panels, lighting panels, balustrades

TYPES / SIZES

4 x 6' (1.2 x 1.8 m), 3/8" (0.95 cm) gauge; satin finish (standard), renewable gloss finish also available

TESTS / EXAMINATIONS

ASTM E84 Class A, NFPA 286 Class A, Light transmitting plastics: CC1

LIMITATIONS

No heat forming or cold bending, single-sided material, 175° F (79.4° C) maximum

CONTACT

3form
2300 West 2300 South
Salt Lake City, UT 84119
Tel: 800-726-0126
www.3-form.com
info@3-form.com

Blob Wall

FREESTANDING MODULAR WALL SYSTEM

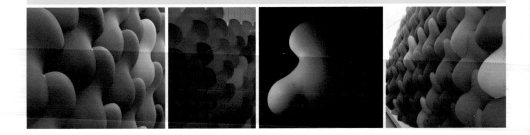

The result of a collaboration between designer Greg Lynn and the principals at Panelite, Blob Wall is an attempt to redefine architecture's most basic building unit—the brick. Blob Wall is a freestanding wall system comprised of a low-density, recyclable, impact-resistant polymer molded into colorful modular units using computer numerical control (CNC) technology.

Each brick, or "blob unit," is a trilobed hollow shape that is mass produced through rotational molding. Using sophisticated software, individual blob units are intersected to form a freestanding wall, allowing for an endless number of prefabricated configurations and custom applications.

The Blob Wall debuted at Skin + Bones: Parallel Practices in Architecture and Fashion at the Los Angeles Museum of Contemporary Art in November 2006 and was also shown at Art Basel, Switzerland, in June 2007.

CONTENTS
Linear low-density
polyethylene (LLDPE)

APPLICATIONS
Spatial divider or sculptural
installation for exterior or
interior applications

TYPES / SIZES
6 standard designs, 6 color
schemes; 18'7" x 2'3" x 9' (5.7
x .7 x 2.7 m); custom wall
configurations
and color combinations
available

ENVIRONMENTAL
Recyclable, may be
produced using recycled
material (dark colors only),
efficient use of material:
wall thickness is 1/8"
(.32 cm)

LIMITATIONS
Not fire-rated, not intended
for load-bearing
applications

CONTACT
Panelite
5835 Adams Boulevard
Culver City, CA 90232
Tel: 323-297-0115
www.panelite.us
blobwall@panelite.us

Brick

LASER-CUT-POLYSTYRENE MODULE SHELVING

Ronan & Erwan Bouroullec's Brick modules are laser-cut-polystyrene shelving units. Originally conceived for the backdrop for an exhibition, the Brick system represents an idea for a new, upscaled iteration of the common building unit. The modules are designed to be easy to assemble and capable of being adapted to various configurations. The Bouroullecs selected polystyrene-cutting as the mode of production in part because of its international ubiquity; Brick may therefore be manufactured on demand near the sites of use.

CONTENTS
Polystyrene

APPLICATIONS
Storage, display unit,
spatial divider

TYPES / SIZES
19.7 x 118.1 x 15.7" (50 x
300 x 40 cm)

ENVIRONMENTAL
Manufacturing method
reduces transportation cost

CONTACT
Ronan & Erwan Bouroullec
23 Rue du Buisson
Saint-Louis
75010 Paris
France
Tel: +33 1-42-00-40-33
www.bouroullec.com
info@bouroullec.com

Chroma

CAST PMMA RESIN

Chroma is a solid, horizontally recyclable cast polymethyl methacrylate (PMMA) resin surface infused with color. Developed by 3form in collaboration with Bayer Material Science, Chroma offers unusually rich and highly saturated integral hues that will not scratch off. It has a renewable matte finish, allowing the material to be resurfaced to like-new condition.

CONTENTS

Cast polymethyl methacrylate (PMMA) with organic dyed surface

APPLICATIONS

Interior horizontal surfaces, such as bar tops, desk tops, vanity and work surfaces

TYPES / SIZES

1/2" (1.3 cm) gauge: 4 x 8' (1.2 x 2.4 m), 4 x 10' (1.2 x 3 m); 1" (2.5 cm) gauge: 2 x 8' (0.6 x 2.4 m), 4 x 8' (1.2 x 2.4 m), 4 x 10' (1.2 x 3 m)

ENVIRONMENTAL

Engineered for horizontal recycling and downstream flexibility, supported by the 3form reclaim program

TESTS / EXAMINATIONS

Light transmitting plastics—CC2 by ASTM D635

LIMITATIONS

Not for exterior use (UV stable options available); maximum use temperature not to exceed 200°F (93.3°C)

CONTACT

3form
2300 West 2300 South
Salt Lake City, UT 84119
Tel: 800-726-0126
www.3-form.com
info@3-form.com

Clampology

A COLLECTION OF AD HOC FUNCTIONAL OBJECTS

Clampology is a family of informal objects designed to increase functionality of interior spaces. Manufactured by London-based designer Jorre van Ast, the collection of adaptive utensils for the domestic environment includes a bookend accompanied by a "book finger," a book display, a hook and a rail that clamp onto the side of horizontal surfaces, a hook to clamp onto electrical pipes, a candle holder, and a cable manager that can be clamped onto a table leg.

CONTENTS
Plastic, spring steel

APPLICATIONS
Display, storage, support

TYPES / SIZES
Types include clamp-a-book, clamp-a-hook, clamp-a-cable; sizes range from 2 x 3 7/8 x 1" (5 x 10 x 2.5 cm) to 3 7/8 x 11 13/16 x 1 3/4" (10 x 30 x 4.5 cm)

CONTACT
Jorre van Ast
35 Bentley Road
London N1 4BY
United Kingdom
Tel: +44 (0)20-8880-0690
www.jorrevanast.com
info@jorrevanast.com

HONEYCOMB COMPOSITE PANEL

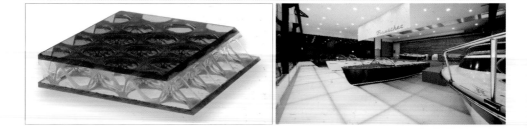

Austria-based Design Composite's TRIcore honeycomb technology allows for the manufacture of panels with exceptional light transmittance relative to their high structural strength. Clear-PEP panels are made of transparent thermoplastic top sheets bonded to rigid translucent cores and are produced in five varieties differing in top sheet material and structure, dimensions, and colors.

Produced in one of the world's largest and most advanced flatbed lamination plants using a variety of polycarbonate and polymethyl methacrylate (PMMA) coatings, Clear-PEP panels offer excellent light scattering, translucent optics, thermal insulation, impact-resistance, exceptional stiffness, as well as low weight.

CONTENTS
Polycarbonate, acrylic

APPLICATIONS
Exterior applications, interior design, shop fitting, exhibitions, events

TYPES / SIZES
Clear-PEP PC, clear-PEP UV PC, clear-PEP UV PC color, clear-PEP UV satin, clear-PEP UV PC stage; 100 3/8 x 41 5/16 x 5/8 / 3/4" (255 x 105 x 1.6/1.9 cm), 118 7/8 x 48 x 3/4" (302 x 122 x 1.9 cm), 118 7/8 x 39 3/8 x 3/4" (302 x 100 x 1.9 cm); panel size up to 307 1/16 x 79 1/2 x 5 7/8" (780 x 202 x 15 cm)

ENVIRONMENTAL
100% recyclable

TESTS / EXAMINATIONS
Fire class B1-ÖNORM B 3800, 1Y-BS 476 Part 7

LIMITATIONS
Not thermoformable, flat applications only

CONTACT
Design Composite GmbH
Klausgasse 32
5730 Mittersill
Austria
Tel: +43-6562-40609-0
www.design-composite
.com
info@design-composite
.com

CoreTough

CLOSED-CELL HONEYCOMB CORE PANELS

CoreTough is a composite panel that gets its strength from a structural honeycomb of various polymers. Manufactured by Transportation Systems Solutions using a proprietary core-forming process, CoreTough is lighter than most other structural panel materials and stronger than many honeycomb composites. The recyclable plastic core is highly resistant to damage by impact and is also impervious to rust, corrosion, rot, biodegradation, mold, and swelling.

CONTENTS
Polycarbonate, polypropylene, high-impact polystyrene, acrylonitrile butadiene styrene (ABS)

APPLICATIONS
Transportation-vehicle construction panels, building panel cores, door cores, furniture

TYPES / SIZES
4 x 8' (1.2 x 2.4 m), 4 x 10' (1.2 x 3 m), 8 x 20' (2.4 x 6.1 m), 10 x 20' (3 x 6.1 m)

ENVIRONMENTAL
100% recyclable, can be made from reground material

TESTS / EXAMINATIONS
FMVSS-302; ASTM C518-85, C364-61, C365-57, C384

LIMITATIONS
Maximum size 10 x 20' (3 x 6.1 m)

CONTACT
Transportation Systems Solutions LLC
255 Swathmore Avenue
High Point, NC 27263
Tel: 336-841-0050
www.tss-llc.com
sales@tss-llc.com

POROUS, STRUCTURAL, USER-ADJUSTED MODULAR WALL SYSTEM

Drapewall is a full-scale wall prototype that explores energy conservation, modular-component assembly, and prefabricated construction for an inexpensive house. Designed by Marc Swackhamer and Blair Satterfield of slvDESIGN, Drapewall is assembled quickly via the stacking of high-strength, low-weight exterior modules, which are held in place by interlocking interior modules. A pattern of clear openings permits light into the house interior. The modules can be configured to face the sun, reducing electric-lighting requirements. Holes along the entire length of the wall system open to allow for natural ventilation, reducing cooling costs. Portions of the wall can also be used for storage, thus minimizing the floor area.

A quiltlike fabric on the interior surface of the wall creates an interactive weather seal. Through the interplay between the hard outer shell and soft inner fabric, the homeowner can control the interior environment in response to outside conditions, such as temperature, humidity, precipitation, light levels, and desired views. The quilt is comprised of multiple layers of materials. Some layers keep water out, others provide insulation, and others provide a soft, acoustically absorbant surface that homeowners can customize with colors and patterns according to personal taste. The fabric also incorporates waterproof zippers for opening and closing specific pockets of the wall.

CONTENTS

Aluminum modular frame, vacuum-formed polyethylene terephthalate (PET) and polystyrene (PS) plastic panels, recycled industrial wool felt, waterproof zippers

APPLICATIONS

Low-cost residential construction

TYPES / SIZES

32 x 16 x 8" (81.3 x 40.6 x 20.3 cm)

ENVIRONMENTAL

Increases ventilation, reduces energy consumption

LIMITATIONS

Currently limited to single-story application

CONTACT

slvDESIGN
89 Church Street SE
Minneapolis, MN 55455
Tel: 612-626-0105
www.slvdesign.com

Flame-Retardant Bioplastic

NONTOXIC FIRE-RETARDING POLYMERS

Plastics used for the external casing of medium-sized and larger electronic equipment, such as personal computers, require a high degree of flame retardancy. To make typical plastics flame resistant, substances with flame-retardant properties, such as halogen and phosphorous compounds, are used as additives. However, halogen compounds expel environmentally damaging toxins when burned; phosphorus compounds, commonly used as substitutes for halogen compounds, are also feared to be toxic.

After creating a flame-retardant polycarbonate resin with a silicone additive called Ekoporika, NEC developed a self-extinguishing epoxy resin compound as a molding material for electronic components such as IC packages. This compound does not require any flame-retarding additive because the resin itself forms a thermally insulating foam layer when exposed to flames.

NEC's research has since expanded to include the development of fire-retardant polylactic acid (PLA) polymers, which are derived from corn rather than petroleum. These plastics utilize the primary flame-retarding ingredient, metal hydroxide, which is a natural component of soil, as well as other environmentally safe additives.

CONTENTS
Polycarbonate resin, epoxy resin, or polylactic acid (PLA)

APPLICATIONS
Computers, electronics, packaging for sensitive equipment

TYPES / SIZES
Custom

ENVIRONMENTAL
Environmentally safe alternatives to halogen or phosphorous

CONTACT
NEC Corporation
7-1, Shiba 5 Chome,
Minato-ku
Tokyo 108-8001
Japan
Tel: +81 (03) 3454-3388
www.nec.com

Flextegrity

STRUCTURED POLYHEDRAL GEOTEXTILE

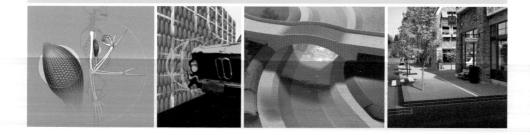

Flextegrity utilizes digital geometric modeling to create structural geotextiles and dimensional meshes at a variety of scales. Interlocking polyhedral shapes are constructed with polymers, metals, or other materials. The geometries employed are naturally superior in structural compression, and the individual modules are suspended and secured within an anisotropic, multiaxial web that resists omnidirectional forces. Applied forces may cause slight local deformation, but the system resists these forces as a larger, integrated assembly.

While each polyhedral unit is a static object with basic properties, the assembled system behaves like a flexible fabric that can be finely tuned to match complex topographies. The porosity of the mesh also yields an assembly that is permeable without sacrificing structural integrity. According to the manufacturer, Flextegrity is suitable for the construction of load-bearing three-dimensional materials, flexible structural blocks, and hybrid material sheets.

CONTENTS
Recycled polymers, biopolymers, fiber-reinforced polymers, metals

APPLICATIONS
Structural geotextiles for stormwater management, permeable paving, preassembled sidewalks with integrated drainage and lighting, disaster-resistant building construction

TYPES / SIZES
Scalable

ENVIRONMENTAL
Efficient use of material, mitigates storm-water runoff, recycled content, recyclable

CONTACT
Flextegrity Inc.
1720 NW Lovejoy, Box 224
Portland, OR 97209
Tel: 503-253-0853
www.flextegrity.com
marketing@flextegrity.com

Geometric Structure Cushions

N° 124516-001

SHAPE-MEMORY EVA-FOAM STRUCTURE

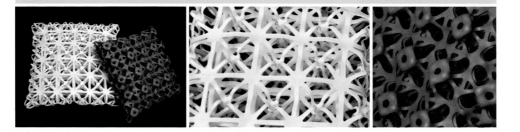

Geometric Structure Cushions are porous skeletal structures that can be flattened and then returned to their original form. Developed by London-based Lauren Moriarty using digital-fabrication techniques, each structure is designed virtually before it is laser cut and hand finished. The cushions are flame resistant and are fabricated in a variety of colors and three-dimensional patterns.

CONTENTS

Ethylene vinyl acetate
(EVA) foam

APPLICATIONS

Cushioning properties,
aesthetic applications

TYPES / SIZES

4.7 in² (30 cm²), 5.4 in²
(35 cm²), custom sizes

ENVIRONMENTAL

Manufactured using a low-impact nitrogen-expansion technique

LIMITATIONS

Not for exterior use

CONTACT

Lauren Moriarty
Studio W8, Cockpit Studios,
Northington Street
London WC1N 2NP
United Kingdom
Tel: +44(0)7787 562533
www.laurenmoriarty.co.uk
info@laurenmoriarty.co.uk

Illusion Flex

N° 097216-002

3D OPTICAL FILM FOR SOLID AND TRANSLUCENT SURFACES

Creative Environments produces an optical film made of vinyl or polycarbonate intended to visually enhance horizontal and vertical interior surfaces, including countertops, floors, and feature walls. Rigid surfaces call for polycarbonate-based film, while flexible surfaces are made of vinyl.

Similar to the reflective-technology concept used in license plates and highway signage, thousands of optical lenses are embedded into the surface of Illusion Flex film. While this technology can seem flat in its appearance, Illusion Flex conveys an impression of depth, akin to a radiant metallic fabric, compressed into a flat plane. The apparent three-dimensionality of the film changes with the direction and type of lighting used, and reflected light intensifies this effect. Illusion Flex is available in a variety of colors and patterns.

CONTENTS
Polycarbonate or vinyl

APPLICATIONS
Walls (solid or translucent),
ceilings, floors, counters,
tables, column surrounds

TYPES / SIZES
20 colors, 5 patterns;
translucent or opaque

TESTS / EXAMINATIONS
Class 1 fire-rated (optional)

LIMITATIONS
Maximum width 25 3/8"
(64.5 cm)

CONTACT
Creative Environments
1009 Villa Lane
Boynton Beach, FL 33435
Tel: 561-369-1900
www.ilusionflex.com
ken@illusionflex.com

Intelligent Bioplastic

RECYCLABLE SHAPE-MEMORY BIOPOLYMER

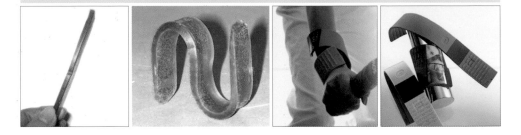

Unlike conventional petroleum-based plastics, polylactic acid (PLA) plastic is mass produced by chemical synthesis using raw materials derived from corn. The production of PLA contributes less CO_2 to the atmosphere than that of conventional plastics and offers superior biodegradability after disposal. Because PLA plastics are often more expensive than conventional ones, researchers are developing ways to add value to PLA plastics.

NEC Corporation's Dr. Masatoshi Iji has developed a PLA-based bioplastic with shape memory and recyclability. The polymer deforms with heat and external pressure and remains in that altered shape when cooled. Once reheated, the plastic returns to its original shape. Shape memory conventionally requires plastics with a cross-linked structure, which prohibits melting and thus recycling. However, NEC's shape-memory polymer utilizes a characteristic called thermoreversible cross-linking. The material can be deformed and restored to its original shape by heating at the temperature of a hairdryer (approx. 140°F [60°C]), but if heated to a typical molding temperature 320°F (160°C) the cross-linked structure dissociates, causing the material to melt and enabling easy recyclability.

This recyclable, shape-memory bioplastic allows users to deform the material into any shape, making possible all kinds of new products and applications, like futuristic wearable electronic equipment.

CONTENTS
Polylactic acid (PLA) polymer

APPLICATIONS
Shapable mobile electronic devices, wearable computing, moldable furnishings

TYPES / SIZES
Custom

ENVIRONMENTAL
Non-petroleum-based polymer, horizontal recyclability

CONTACT
NEC Corporation
7-1, Shiba 5 Chome, Minato-ku
Tokyo 108-8001
Japan
Tel: +81 (03) 3454-3388
www.nec.com

Kenaf-Reinforced Bioplastic

PLA POLYMER REINFORCED WITH KENAF FIBERS

The current rapid depletion of petroleum resources has led to the search for renewable alternatives. One response is the development of bioplastic, made of plant-derived materials (biomass). A substitute for petroleum-based materials, biomass-based materials have distinct advantages, such as the ability to reduce the CO_2 gas that causes global warming and superior degradability (biodegradability) in the soil after disposal.

Dr. Masatoshi Iji and his laboratory at NEC Corporation have developed a new composite material comprised of kenaf fiber–reinforced polylactic acid. With a 90 percent biomass content, it boasts the highest biomass-based content of any current bioplastic material used for electronic equipment. Kenaf is a plant originally grown in Africa, with one of the highest rates of CO_2 absorption of any plant. (Its photosynthesis rate is 3 to 9 times higher than that of ordinary plants resins, and it is capable of absorbing approximately 1.4 tons of CO_2 per ton.) It is very effective in mitigating the effects of global warming and is currently being grown on other continents for its beneficial properties.

Kenaf-Reinforced Bioplastic was recently used for the casing of a Japanese mobile phone, which was the first phone in the world with a casing made mostly of bioplastic. The casing was produced without thick pigments or additional coatings, subtly revealing the kenaf fibers.

CONTENTS
Polylactic acid (PLA), kenaf fibers

APPLICATIONS
Mobile electronics, computer casings, automotive components, product design

TYPES / SIZES
Custom

ENVIRONMENTAL
Utilizes nonpetroleum based materials, rapidly renewable biofiber

CONTACT
NEC Corporation
7-1, Shiba 5 Chome,
Minato-ku
Tokyo 108-8001
Japan
Tel: +81 (03) 3454-3388
www.nec.com

L-8100

HEAT-CURED EPOXY ADHESIVE TAPE

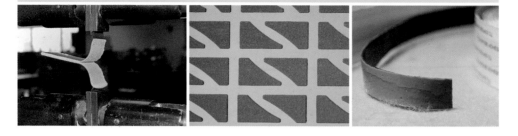

The L-8100 series heat-cured structural adhesive tape can be used to replace resistance welds and mechanical fasteners to visually improve critical show surfaces on metal office furniture, household appliances, and automobiles. This product can often reduce cost by eliminating time-consuming drill and rivet operations. L-8100 is also more consistent, provides higher strength, eliminates waste and cleanup operations compared to pumpable adhesives. Moreover, L-8100 can be used to reduce local stress concentrations that lead to fatigue cracking and premature product failure.

Supplied as rolls or unique die-cut shapes, L-8100 is formulated to adhere to oily metal surfaces. Additionally, this product can be supplied with one nontacky side for ease of handling and application, which may be performed either manually or through automation. L-8100 is resistant to all types of phosphate and phosphoric-acid cleaning solutions as well as mineral and vanishing oils commonly found on sheet metal.

CONTENTS
Epoxy resins, blowing agent

APPLICATIONS
Structurally bonding metal with nonmetal components

TYPES / SIZES
Available on rolls or unique die-cut shapes

ENVIRONMENTAL
Eliminates waste and cleanup typical of liquid and paste adhesives, cured product gives off no volatile organic compounds

TESTS / EXAMINATIONS
Peel test ASTM D-1876, Lap shear SAE J1523v001

LIMITATIONS
End use product temperature should not exceed 176°F (80°C), five-month shelf life

CONTACT
LL Products
160 Mclean Drive
Romeo, MI 48065
Tel: 586-336-1701
www.llproducts.com
contact@llproducts.com

HEAT-CURED-COMPOSITE PANEL-EDGE FINISH MATERIAL

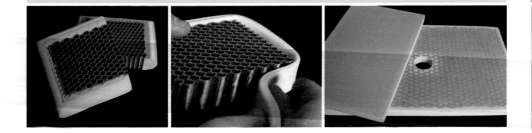

Honeycomb structural panels are currently widely used in a variety of industries, such as aerospace and building construction, for their light weight and rigidity. While panel surfaces typically require no protection, edges are often a problem because the internal structure is exposed.

The L-9000 series heat-cured composite materials save time and labor over traditional two-part paste-type applications for honeycomb-panel edges. Being a pliable tape, L-9000 can be applied quickly and easily to composite honeycomb panels. Oven curing this product at a range of 250 to 275°F (121 to 135°C) provides a volume expansion from 100 to 400 percent. This versatility allows for filling gaps and providing an edge that can machined to optimal fit and finish specifications.

The predictable post-cure density provides uniform material specifications in finished panels and can be saw cut, laser cut, milled, sanded, or lathed to meet demanding fit and finish requirements.

CONTENTS
Epoxy resin, blowing agent

APPLICATIONS
Honeycomb-panel edge finishing

TYPES / SIZES
Wide variety of strip widths

ENVIRONMENTAL
Eliminates waste and cleanup typical of two-part liquid and paste materials, cured product gives off no volatile organic compounds

TESTS / EXAMINATIONS
Burn AITM 2.0002A, Smoke Density FAR 25.853(D) & ASTM F 814(FM), Toxicity AITM 3.0005/ABD 0031/ FMO, Tube shear strength DIN EN 2667-2

LIMITATIONS
End-use product temperature should not exceed 176°F (80°C)

CONTACT
LL Products
160 Mclean Drive
Romeo, MI 48065
Tel: 586-336-1701
www.llproducts.com
contact@llproducts.com

Lumi-Line

PHOSPHORESCENT FIBER-REINFORCED PLASTIC

The depth of designer Kazuko Akamatsu's Lumi-Line tabletop is only an eighth of an inch (.3 centimeters), thanks to engineering ingenuity and a synergistic combination of materials. Akamatsu adhered bundled fiberglass threads to a nonstructural, translucent plastic sheet with a translucent liquid glue. The pattern of the reinforcing "strings" is not random, but rather the result of a structural study to determine how to construct the thinnest tabletop possible. The table surface, reinforcing, and legs all act together as one system in order to resist loads and allow the legs to be placed away from "expected" locations.

While Lumi-Line allows light to pass through its milky surface by day, it assumes an entirely different character at night. Akamatsu imbued the fiber strands with phosphorescence, thus rendering the strings as sharp glowing lines floating midair in the dark.

CONTENTS
Fiber-reinforced plastic

APPLICATIONS
Table

TYPES / SIZES
31 1/2 x 31 1/2 x 1/8" (80 x 80 x .3 cm); custom sizes available

CONTACT
CAt (C and A tokyo)
1-20-5-4F, Ebisu-Nishi,
Shibuya-ku
Tokyo 150-0021
Japan
Tel: +81 (03) 5489-8264
www.c-and-a.co.jp
info@c-and-a.co.jp

Plastic

FLEXIBLE WEDGE SHELVING SYSTEM

Make/Shift is a flexible shelving system that can be arranged to fill spaces of varying sizes and between walls or even pillars. The interlocking wedge shape of the units allows them to "expand" or "contract" within a space: a single pair may be used for small gaps, or multiple modules may be linked together to make larger units.

Conceived by Peter Marigold, Make/Shift was designed for frequent movers who often encounter difficulties adapting their existing furniture to new settings. The shelves easily conform to any space larger than 19 7/32 inches (48.8 centimeters), the width of a single module. Make/Shift units may also be assembled into freestanding units using the clips provided.

Make/Shift is fabricated in black, white, and pink Arpro expanded polypropylene (EPP), which is a lightweight, steam-cleanable foam that is stronger and more resilient than expanded polystyrene (EPS). Arpro also recycles the CO_2 emitted in the manufacture of the material, which may also be recycled at the end of its life. Make/Shift is available from Movisi.

INTELLIGENT PRODUCT

CONTENTS
Arpro expanded
polypropylene (EPP)

APPLICATIONS
Storage, spatial divider

TYPES / SIZES
Black, white, or pink; 44
13/32 x 19 7/32 x 12 13/16"
(112.8 x 48.8 x 32.5 cm)

ENVIRONMENTAL
Recyclable, CO_2 recycled
during manufacture, light
weight reduces
transportation costs

LIMITATIONS
Not recommended for
extended outdoor use
(UV exposure)

CONTACT
Movisi
Industriestrasse 27
Wieslendorfer Strasse 48
74182 Obersulm-Eschenau
Germany
www.movisi.com
info@movisi.com

Mind the Gap

THREE-DIMENSIONAL ACRYLIC WALLPAPER

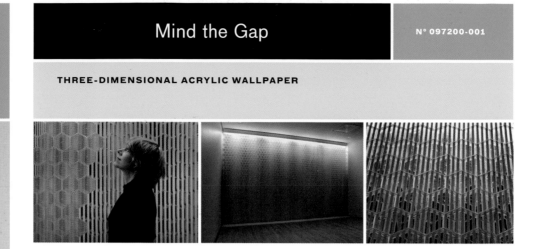

Mind the Gap is an interconnected network of acrylic hexagonal boxes and strips applied in varying densities. Designer Ane Lykke uses these boxes as bricks to construct custom walls with specific depths and perspectives. The parallel layers and reflections on the acrylic surfaces create optical illusions in which the strips appear to move depending at the viewer's position and proximity to the wall. Therefore, light and the movement of the spectator "alter" the pattern of the wall, conjuring a living, vibrating surface.

CONTENTS
Acrylic

APPLICATIONS
Wall surfacing, art
installation

TYPES / SIZES
Custom

LIMITATIONS
Not for exterior use

CONTACT
Ane Lykke
Stockholmsgade 53 kld.
2100 Copenhagen
Denmark
Tel: +45 2425-2849
www.anelykke.com
mind@anelykke.com

Noodle Block Cube

3D CELLULAR SHAPE-MEMORY STRUCTURE

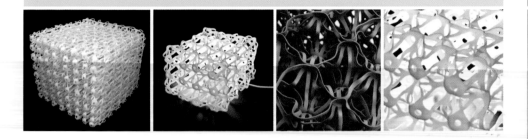

Lauren Moriarty's Noodle Block Cubes represent intriguing experiments in digitally fabricated three-dimensional cellular structures that may be compressed and also reverted to their original form. Moriarty designs the pieces in a digital environment, and they are then laser cut and hand finished. The cubes may be used as decorative seats, cushions, sculpture, or playthings.

CONTENTS
Ethylene-vinyl acetate (EVA) foam

APPLICATIONS
Seating, cushion, sculpture

TYPES / SIZES
2.4 in³ (40 cm³), 3.7 in³ (60 cm³), custom sizes and colors

ENVIRONMENTAL
Manufactured using a low-impact-nitrogen expansion technique

LIMITATIONS
Not for exterior use

CONTACT
Lauren Moriarty
Studio W8, Cockpit Studios,
Northington Street
London WC1N 2NP
United Kingdom
+44(0)7787 562533
www.laurenmoriarty.co.uk
info@laurenmoriarty.co.uk

RECOMBINANT PRODUCT

Organics

LAMINATED VIRGIN AND 40% POSTINDUSTRIAL RECYCLED PETG

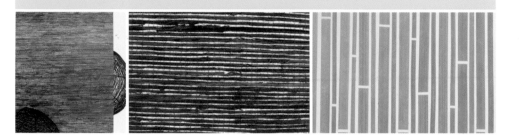

To make Organics, 3form laminates various organic materials between sheets of partially recycled polyethylene terephthalate glycol (PETG) obtained from postindustrial sources. The company collaborates closely with artisans in Nepal, Vietnam, and Indonesia to select and process materials such as bamboo and banana fibers. These materials are first prepared using techniques such as mud drying and thin, linear slicing to create various colors and shapes. These fibers are then incorporated between panels of Ecoresin, which contains 40 percent recycled content.

CONTENTS
Polyethylene terephthalate glycol modified (PETG), organic interlayer

APPLICATIONS
Vertical and horizontal surfaces, furniture, lighting, signage, acoustics

TYPES / SIZES
4 x 8' (1.2 x 2.4 m), 4 x 10' (1.2 x 3 m); custom sizes available; multiple finishes available

ENVIRONMENTAL
GreenGuard Certified for indoor air quality.

TESTS / EXAMINATIONS
ASTM E84: 1/4 to 3/4" (.6 to 1.9 cm) gauges = CLASS B, 1" (2.5 cm) gauge = CLASS A; NFPA 286: 1/4 to 3/8" (.6 to .95 cm) gauges = CLASS A

LIMITATIONS
Maximum temperature use 150° F (65.6° C); requires UV protection and edge sealing for exterior use

CONTACT
3form
2300 West 2300 South
Salt Lake City, UT 84119
Tel: 800-726-0126
www.3-form.com
info@3-form.com

Power Plastic

ENERGY-HARNESSING POLYMER FILM

Konarka's Power Plastic converts light to energy and can be integrated into any device, system, or structure that is exposed to light. Power Plastic is based on organic photovoltaic (OPV) technology and is extremely lightweight and flexible. OPVs are thin films comprised of multiple nanostructured layers of semiconducting organic materials and are predicted to revolutionize the solar energy industry because they can be fabricated using low-cost, mass-production-solution-based processes such as ink-jet or screen printing.

Power Plastic utilizes a wider range of the light spectrum than conventional solar cells and allows all visible light sources to be used to generate power. The film easily conforms to a variety of product-design applications and may be customized with various colors and shapes.

CONTENTS
Organic photovoltaic (OPV)

APPLICATIONS
Power generation

TYPES / SIZES
Custom

ENVIRONMENTAL
Low-cost power generation
from all visible light

CONTACT
Konarka
116 John Street, Suite 12,
3rd Floor
Lowell, MA 01852
Tel: 978-569-1407
www.konarka.com
jbraman@konarka.com

Precious Cargo

THERMAL PACKAGING UTILIZING EPP AND VACUUM-INSULATION TECHNOLOGY

Precious Cargo is a compact, hygienic, and insulated container technology for the safe transportation of temperature-sensitive goods. Designed by Naomi Tsai and manufactured by va-Q-tec, Precious Cargo has a vacuum insulating panel (VIP) interior and a lightweight, shock-absorbing outer casing for additional protection.

VIPs are made of open-pore particles vacuum-packed with high-barrier metallized multilayer films and represent the next wave of superior insulation technology. The thermal performance of Precious Cargo is up to fifteen times higher than that of conventional cases.

CONTENTS

Expanded polypropylene (EPP) outer casing, vacuum insulation panels (VIP), polypropylene inner lining, cool packs

APPLICATIONS

Long-haul transportation and intermediate storage of temperature-sensitive goods for biomedical, pharmaceutical, and food and beverage applications

TYPES / SIZES

Outer dimension: 15 3/4 x 15 3/4 x 9 7/8" (40 x 40 x 25 cm), inner dimension: 13 3/8 x 13 3/8 x 6 9/32" (34 x 34 x 16 cm); internal capacity 18.5 L (4.9 Gal)

ENVIRONMENTAL

Recyclable

TESTS / EXAMINATIONS

Technical information available upon request

LIMITATIONS

Although the interior can sustain temperatures up to 1652°F (900°C) without damage, the outer plastic barrier film disintegrates at temperatures above 302 to 392°F (150 to 200°C); high humidity may be harmful to VIPs

CONTACT

va-Q-tec AG
Karl-Ferdinand-Braun-Str. 7
D-97080 Würzburg
Germany
Tel: +49 (0) 931-35-942-0
www.va-q-tec.com
info@va-q-tec.com

TRANSPARENT METAL-FREE WINDOW FILM

Traditional window films peel, bubble, corrode, and leave a metallic glare on windows. 3M, however, has developed the first clear, metal-free window film. The Prestige series blocks up to 99.9 percent of ultraviolet rays, rejects 63 percent of solar heat, and even holds together glass shattered during hurricanes. Prestige film will not darken windows like traditional films.

Constructed using a combination of nanoparticles and polyester films that are over 200 layers thick, the Prestige series film is actually thinner than a Post-it note. The film utilizes the optical properties present in the layers of nanoparticles, allowing light from the visible spectrum to pass through while deflecting ultraviolet and infrared wavelengths. The Prestige series also contains a specially engineered adhesive that is guaranteed to last the lifetime of the window.

CONTENTS
Multilayered polymers

APPLICATIONS
Ultraviolet ray blocking, heat rejection, increased safety from broken glass

TYPES / SIZES
Fits windows of all sizes

ENVIRONMENTAL
Reduces energy use

LIMITATIONS
Must be professionally installed

CONTACT
3M
3M Center, Building
223-03-S-24
St. Paul, MN 55144
Tel: 651-733-1455
www.3m.com/prestige
jphanbury@mmm.com

Raydoor

LIGHT-TRANSMITTING MOVEABLE WALLS

Raydoor is a New York–based company that designs and manufactures room-dividing systems for the mid- to upscale residential and commercial interiors market. Responding to the need for daylight transmission within deep floor plates, Raydoor is often fabricated with translucent materials. Raydoor systems are easy to install and operate within most existing conditions. For example, the telescoping, sliding wall requires no floor tracks. Raydoor systems may be installed in sliding-, pocket-, folding-, or fixed-panel configurations and are available in solid as well as light-transmitting formats.

CONTENTS
55% acrylic, 30% medium-density fiberboard (MDF) / wood products, 10% aluminum, 5% laminate

APPLICATIONS
Flexible room division, door

TYPES / SIZES
Standard panel widths 36" (91.4 cm), 41" (104.1 cm), 46" (116.8 cm); standard panel heights 80" (203.2 cm), 92" (233.7 cm), 104" (264.2 cm), 116" (294.6 cm)

ENVIRONMENTAL
Reusable

TESTS / EXAMINATIONS
ASTM 1003, D635 (for acrylic)

LIMITATIONS
Not for exterior use

CONTACT
Raydoor
134 West 29th Street, Suite 909
New York, NY 10001
Tel: 212-421-0641
www.raydoor.com
info@raydoor.com

ETCHED PLASTIC PANELS LAMINATED WITH COLOR-CHANGING FILMS

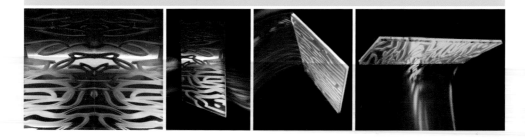

Designed by Naomi Tsai, Revelation Screen combines color-changing film with polycarbonate and acrylic panels etched with organic patterns. Consisting of hundreds of layers of alternating polymers, the thin optical film is highly reflective and transforms from aqua to magenta depending on the viewing angle. The screen can also appear to be a one-way gold mirror, contingent on the lighting employed. The illumination of a specially designed, optional light source intensifies the chromatic effects as well as the shadows.

CONTENTS
Etched polycarbonate or acrylic panels, color-changing polyester film

APPLICATIONS
Panels, screens, wall covering, window treatments, table tops, shelving, light diffuser lenses

TYPES / SIZES
Width 23 5/8" (60 cm)

ENVIRONMENTAL
Recyclable

TESTS / EXAMINATIONS
Technical information available upon request

LIMITATIONS
Not for exterior use

CONTACT
Revelation Lighting
Grosvenor Mill,
Grosvenor Street
Ashton-U-Lyne OL7 0RG
United Kingdom
Tel: +44 (0)161-330-0033
www.revelationlighting
.co.uk
colourillusion@btconnect
.com

Scintilla Lumina

LIGHT-EXTENDING POLYMER-MATRIX PANELS

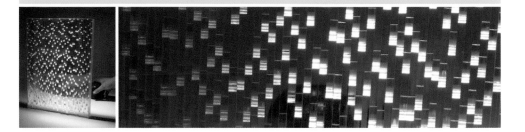

A variation of SensiTile Scintilla, Scintilla Lumina extends light from a single source to hundreds of reflected points along the surface of a material. Constructed of acrylic light pipes, Lumina conveys light along considerable distances in accordance with the same principles that apply to fiber optics. The translucent panel matrix performs as an image "double" for an adjacent object, reflecting the object via the profiles of individual light pipes. Using available LED technology, Scintilla Lumina will actively diffuse and reflect dynamic color sequences beyond 8 linear feet (2.4 meters) in length. Custom-designed panels make possible the integration of graphics, text, and logos.

CONTENTS

100% polymethyl
methacrylate (PMMA)

APPLICATIONS

Interior and exterior panels,
room dividers, light fixtures,
signage, furniture

TYPES / SIZES

4 x 8' (1.2 x 2.4 m) panels,
3/4 and 1 1/4" (1.9 and 3.1
cm) thick; flexible versions
and custom thicknesses
available

ENVIRONMENTAL

Extends efficacy of low-
energy light sources,
recyclable material

CONTACT

SensiTile Systems
1604 Clay Avenue, 3rd Floor
Detroit, MI 48211
Tel: 313-872-6314
www.sensitile.com
info@sensitile.com

FLEXIBLE POLYPROPYLENE AND POLYCARBONATE SHELVING SYSTEM

Ronan & Erwan Bouroullec's Self is a modular display cabinet comprised by simple, playful elements. White or black polypropylene shelves are stacked vertically using transparent polycarbonate support panels in multiple colors. Self may be built quickly in various configurations without the need for tools. The shelving can be open, closed, or accessed from both sides and can function as a bookshelf, display cabinet, or room divider. Self can even be configured in "bridge" configurations, spanning over partitions or creating voids for taller objects. In this way, Self approaches the ultimate state of flexibility.

CONTENTS
Blown polypropylene, polycarbonate, galvanized steel

APPLICATIONS
Display shelving, storage, space divider

TYPES / SIZES
Heights 19 3/4" (50.2 cm), 35 1/2" (90.2 cm), 51 1/4" (130.2 cm), or 67" (170.2 cm)

CONTACT
Vitra
Klünenfeldstrasse 22
CH-4127 Birsfelden
Switzerland
Tel: +41 61-377-0000
www.vitra.com
info@vitra.com

Self-Healing Polymers

N° 065000-002

A STRUCTURAL POLYMERIC MATERIAL WITH THE ABILITY TO AUTONOMICALLY HEAL CRACKS

Structural polymers are susceptible to damage: cracks form deep within the structure where detection is difficult and repair is almost impossible. Damage in polymeric coatings, adhesives, microelectronic components, and structural composites can span many length scales. Structural composites subject to impact loading can sustain significant damage on centimeter length scales, which in turn can lead to subsurface millimeter scale delaminations and micron-scale matrix cracking. Coatings and microelectronic packaging components have cracks that initiate on even smaller scales. Once cracks have formed within polymeric materials, the integrity of the structure is significantly compromised.

Inspired by biological systems in which damage triggers a healing response, Scott White at the Beckman Institute at the University of Illinois developed a structural polymeric material with the ability to autonomically heal cracks. The incorporation of a microencapsulated healing agent and a catalytic chemical trigger within an epoxy matrix accomplished this healing process. An approaching crack ruptures embedded microcapsules, releasing healing agent into the crack plane through capillary action. Polymerization is triggered by contact with the embedded catalyst, bonding the crack faces.

CONTENTS
Polymer matrix, microencapsulated healing agent, catalytic chemical trigger

APPLICATIONS
A wide variety of applications ranging from microelectronics to aerospace, including polymeric coatings, adhesives, and structural composites

ENVIRONMENTAL
Extended life of commercial products

CONTACT
Beckman Institute
University of Illinois
3361 Beckman Institute
405 North Mathews Avenue
Urbana, IL 61801
www.autonomic.uiuc.edu

LIGHT-BENDING POLYMER CUBE

SensiTile S90 is a light-bending polymer cube that acts as a 90-degree mirror, transferring images of adjacent objects precisely across surfaces. A matrix of carefully placed, rectangular acrylic light pipes, S90 produces a corresponding image in a "pixelated" version in which the thickness of the pipes determines the visual resolution. S90 is offered as a standard 6-inch (15.2 centimeter) cube and is being developed for use as a building module or infrastructural unit, such as a safety-enhancing street curb.

CONTENTS

100% polymethyl
methacrylate (PMMA)

APPLICATIONS

Exterior or interior wall
module, flooring, stairs,
light fixtures, signage,
street curbs

TYPES / SIZES

6 in³ (15.2 cm³) cube;
custom sizes available

ENVIRONMENTAL

Extends efficacy of low-
energy light sources,
recyclable material

CONTACT

SensiTile Systems
1604 Clay Avenue, 3rd Floor
Detroit, MI 48211
Tel: 313-872-6314
www.sensitile.com
info@sensitile.com

SkinBag

BAGS AND GARMENTS MADE OF SYNTHETIC HUMAN SKIN

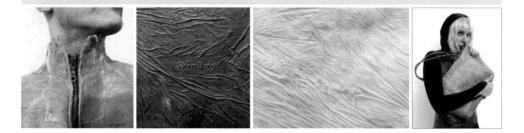

SkinBag is a range of clothing and accessories fabricated from synthetic human skin. The skin is latex that is molded with creases and a texture reminiscent of human flesh. SkinBag comes in a variety of colors, the most common of which emulate known values of human skin.

According to the manufacturer, SkinBag is an extension of one's body, a type of discarded skin that retains an identity, "a successful alchemy between the captivating and the repulsive, for a sensual fashion without complacency." Each SkinBag is handcrafted and may be personalized with a tattoo or inscription.

CONTENTS
Caoutchouc rubber (latex)

APPLICATIONS
Bags, garments,
accessories, wall coverings

TYPES / SIZES
Various; custom sizes
available

ENVIRONMENTAL
Recyclable

CONTACT
SkinBag
3, Impasse de la Pierre
Boisset les Prévanches
27120 France
www.skinbag.net
info@skinbag.net

Soft Pad

COLORED-URETHANE GEL CUSHION

Soft Pad is a line of simple, playful objects designed by Fabrice Covelli of FProduct to enliven public and private spaces. Each pad is comprised of three distinct layers: The front skin is made of urethane soft resin (Shore hardness 60A) that can consist of a variety of depths, finishes, and colors. The internal gel consists of dyes of different colors and tones, and the back skin is made of urethane soft or hard resin (Shore 60A to 80D) that can also exhibit different colors and thicknesses. These properties can be manipulated for desired aesthetic and structural qualities in wall surfacing, furniture, clothing, and various accessories.

CONTENTS

Soft urethane skin,
urethane gel

APPLICATIONS

Seat cushions, wall tiles,
armrests, headrests,
decorative panels, jewelry,
accessories

TYPES / SIZES

Maximum size 20 x 30"
(50.8 x 76.2 cm)

LIMITATIONS

Not recommended for
intensive public use, not
fire-rated

CONTACT

FProduct
250 Saint Marks Avenue
Brooklyn, NY 11238
www.fproduct.net
getinfo@fproduct.net

Stabiligrid

RECYCLED-PE PERVIOUS-PAVEMENT GRID SYSTEM

Stabiligrid is an economical, easy-to-install, load-bearing pervious-pavement lattice grid. It is an environmentally sound alternative to pavement, effectively reducing storm-water runoff and allowing the underlying soil to absorb and process environmental toxins, such as cadmium, copper, lead, and zinc, and preventing the contamination of groundwater. Stabiligrid also reduces soil erosion, preserving vegetation and natural habitats.

Stabiligrid is lightweight but highly durable, and may be adjusted to fit existing contours using standard tools, such as an angle grinder or circular saw. The grids are typically laid on a 1 to 4 inch (2.5 to 10.2 centimeter) gravel base, depending on the porosity of the substrate below. The grid can be backfilled with gravel, sand, or top soil for vegetated surfaces. The grid facilitates a structural base for green roof systems and reduces both storm-water runoff and the urban heat-island effect.

CONTENTS
100% postconsumer recycled polyethylene (PE)

APPLICATIONS
Roads, driveways, walkways and trails, parking lots, green roof systems, helipads, landscape erosion control, drainage culverts and ditches, construction-site paths, livestock enclosures

TYPES / SIZES
13 1/8 x 13 1/8" (33.3 x 33.3 cm), 1 15/16" (4.9 cm) high

ENVIRONMENTAL
Reduces storm-water runoff, reduces soil erosion, reduces urban heat-island effect, low maintenance

TESTS / EXAMINATIONS
German EPA/EPO, LGA, TUV/Nord, ISO 9001 compliant; certified by BECETEL of Belgium to resist fractures -22 to +158° F (-30 to 70° C); load-bearing capacity of 35.84 tons / ft2 (349,970 kg / m2) when properly installed

LIMITATIONS
Only available in one color (black)

CONTACT
Eco-Terr
9856 Northeast Torvanger Road
Bainbridge Island, WA 98110
Tel: 206-780-1906
www.ecoterr.com
mmccabe@ecoterr.com

Sun-Tec Film

ELECTROCONDUCTIVE POLYESTER FILM WITH EMBEDDED ELECTRONIC DEVICES

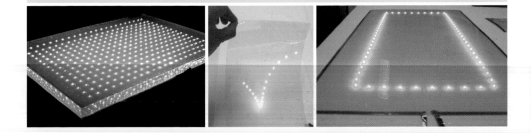

Sun-Tec's electroconductive transparent films contain small mounted electronic devices like LEDs and infrared sensors. Powered by voltages between 12 and 48 VDC, these 125-micron-thick films act as printed circuit boards and may be produced up to 137 3/4 by 49 1/4 inches (350 by 125 centimeters) in single sheets. Applications include windows, floor plates, stairs, tables, and other uses for transparent, illuminated surfaces.

Sun-Tec films may be laminated between glass sheets using UV-curing resin or with vacuum or autoclaving techniques, as temperatures do not exceed 257°F (125°C). The material may also be laminated between polycarbonate or acrylic plates using UV-curing resin or vacuum processes. Sun-Tec films are currently being tested in three-dimensional bent-glass roofs for automotive applications.

CONTENTS
Electroconductive transparent polyester film, embedded electronic devices

APPLICATIONS
Intelligent glass, transparent light-emitting glass

TYPES / SIZES
Maximum size 137 3/4 x 49 1/4" (350 x 125 cm), embedded electronics thickness below 1/64" (0.07 cm), LED and SMD distance > 5/16" (.8 cm)

ENVIRONMENTAL
Low-energy consumption, long life

TESTS / EXAMINATIONS
AC/DC: TÜV EN60950, EMI FCC Part 15 Class B / CISPR-22 Class B

LIMITATIONS
Low voltage applications only (under 48 VDC), maximum current .5 amperes / ft^2 (5 amperes / m^2)

CONTACT
Sun-Tec Swiss United Technologies Co. Ltd.
Rebenweg 20
6331 Hunenberg
Switzerland
Tel: +41 41-740-01-73
www.sun-tec.ch
dshavit@sun-tec.ch

Tide Flowers

TIDAL REGISTER

As landscape artist Stacy Levy reminds us: "nature does not stop in the city." Although most urban rivers exhibit tidal changes, which connect us to the ocean, the moon, and to nature's daily cycle, many urban dwellers are not aware of these transformations. *Tide Flowers* is an installation that registers tidal movement with the simple visual presence of brilliantly colored flowers "blooming" at high tide and "closing" at low tide. *Tide Flowers* is made up of multiple flower units, each with six petals, attached to wooden piles. The petals rise with the tide and also respond to the waves and wakes on the surface of the water.

CONTENTS

Marine vinyl, foam, polycarbonate, stainless-steel hardware

APPLICATIONS

Water-level registration in tidal water bodies

TYPES / SIZES

4' (1.2 m) long petals

ENVIRONMENTAL

Awareness of environmental cycles

TESTS / EXAMINATIONS

Prototype under testing in the New York Harbor

LIMITATIONS

Potential damage by flotsam and ice jams

CONTACT

Sere Ltd.
576 Upper Georges
Valley Road
Spring Mills, PA 16875
Tel: 814-422-8982
www.stacylevy.com
stacylevy@earthlink.net

RECYCLED POLYSTYRENE MOLDING

Timbron interior moldings contain 90 percent recycled polystyrene (75 percent postconsumer) and are processed to have the same density as a soft wood. Easy to install, Timbron may be cut, nailed, fluted, sanded, and painted just like wood. The moldings are durable, waterproof, mold and mildew resistant, and termite proof, and they are also fully recyclable.

CONTENTS
90% recycled-waste plastics (mainly polystyrene), 75% postconsumer content

APPLICATIONS
Interior molding and trim

TYPES / SIZES
Available in 7 common profiles

ENVIRONMENTAL
Recycled content, recyclable, low VOCs, mold and mildew resistant

TESTS / EXAMINATIONS
CA 1350 indoor air-quality testing, Scientific Certification Systems certified, Green Business Certified

LIMITATIONS
Not for exterior use

CONTACT
Timbron
1333 North California Boulevard, #545
Walnut Creek, CA 97596
Tel: 925-943-1632
www.timbron.com
admin@timbron.com

Topo

CUSTOMIZABLE TABLE WITH REMOVABLE PLANTER/VESSELS

Topo is a series of Corian tables with built-in reconfigurable landscapes. Plastic inserts drop into the table to create functional topographies. Topo uses rapid-prototyping technology in a way that enables each table to be different, and customers color in the areas where they want inserts placed in the finished product. These inserts sit in the holes and can be swapped out and rearranged. The little hills and valleys are made of plastic that is formed over real rocks. When not in use, these functional land forms invert to become sculptural mountains. According to designer Scott Franklin, "We spend a lot of time sitting at tables, so it's nice to have some basil planted nearby."

CONTENTS
Dupont Corian, vacuum-
formed styrene, Kydex,
cold-rolled steel, powder
coating

APPLICATIONS
Indoor or outdoor table,
planter, storage

TYPES / SIZES
Large table 96 x 29 x 29"
(243.8 x 73.7 x 73.7 cm),
medium table 72 x 29 x 29"
(182.9 x 73.7 x 73.3 cm),
coffee table 48 x 24 x 15"
(121.9 x 61 x 38.1 cm)

ENVIRONMENTAL
Encourages air-cleansing
plant growth

CONTACT
NONdesigns LLC
620 Moulton Avenue, #112
Los Angeles, CA 90031
Tel: 626-616-0796
www.nondesigns.com
info@nondesigns.com

TEXTURAL POLYPROPYLENE-MODULE WALL SYSTEM

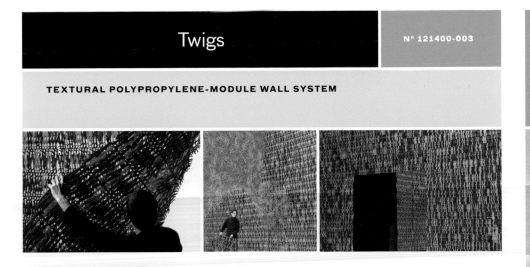

When Ronan & Erwan Bouroullec received a commission to create a rooftop shelter in Paris, they devised a system based on a tiny three-dimensional motif. Like their Algues product, Twigs is comprised by an aggregation of polypropylene units resembling small branches. The Twigs clip together on supporting cables, creating an extensive, irregular, and colorful tapestry. A Twig wall approximates camouflage, with a visual complexity resulting from the repetition of simple units.

CONTENTS
Polypropylene

APPLICATIONS
Screen wall, sculptural installation

TYPES / SIZES
8 1/4 x 3 3/8 x 1" (20.9 x 8.6 x 2.5 cm)

CONTACT
Vitra
Klünenfeldstrasse 22
CH-4127 Birsfelden
Switzerland
Tel: +41 61-377-0000
www.vitra.com
info@vitra.com

Veriflex

TWO-PART SHAPE-MEMORY POLYMER

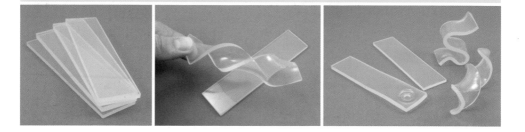

Shape-memory polymers are polymers whose qualities have been altered to give them dynamic shape-memory properties. Under thermal stimuli, shape-memory polymers exhibit a radical change from a rigid polymer to a very elastic state then back to a rigid state again. Veriflex is a patented, two-part, fully formable thermoset shape-memory polymer resin system available for customers to cast into shapes for their distinct applications.

The resin can also be obtained in a cured state in sheets or processed in customers' custom molds. Heated above its activation temperature and in its elastic state, cured Veriflex can be twisted, pulled, bent, and stretched, reaching up to 200 percent elongation. If constrained while cooled, the polymer hardens and can maintain its new deformed configuration indefinitely. When heated above its activation temperature again, this polymer "remembers" or returns to the shape in which it was cured. This process can be repeated indefinitely without loss of the memory shape or degradation of the material.

CONTENTS
Shape-memory polystyrene material

APPLICATIONS
Configurable architecture, shape-changing furniture, customizable molds, shipping and packaging, actuators, rapid manufacturing, thermal sensors

TYPES / SIZES
Standard, thermochromic and custom two-part uncured resins; 1 pint (0.47 L), 1 gallon (3.8 L), 5 gallon (18.9 L), and 55 gallon (208.2 L) units

ENVIRONMENTAL
Reusability and prevention of waste, efficient use of space

TESTS / EXAMINATIONS
ASTM D638, D790, D695, D696

LIMITATIONS
Uncured resins require laboratory and resin handling and curing expertise; thermal activation customizable from −20 to 500° F (−29 to 260° C)

CONTACT
Cornerstone Research Group Industries
2750 Indian Ripple Road
Dayton, OH 45440
Tel: 937-458-0210 x165
www.crgindustries.com
info@crgindustries.com

PETG RESIN ENCAPSULATED PANELS

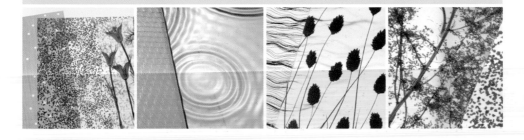

RECOMBINANT MATERIAL

Veritas ResinArt is a fully interchangeable system of colors, patterns, textures, and materials within a multilayered, translucent PETG resin. Designed by Maybeth Shaw and manufactured by Schneller, Veritas is a customizable resin-based panel system—designers can create and order custom samples using a special tool on the Veritas website.

Veritas ResinArt is ideal for a broad range of vertical and horizontal applications, such as doors, ceilings, desktops, and privacy screens. The material may be bent, cut, and fabricated with standard woodworking tools, is Class A fire-rated, and may be a lightweight and cost-effective alternative to glass. Veritas is made with recycled content and is fully recyclable. Moreover, the product is food safe, nontoxic, and manufactured at a solar-powered facility in Florida.

CONTENTS
Glycol-modified polyethylene terephthalate (PETG) resin, varied interlayers

APPLICATIONS
Walls, ceilings, doors, cabinetry, tabletops

TYPES / SIZES
4 x 8' (1.2 x 2.4 m), 4 x 10' (1.2 x 3 m) panels from 1/16 to 1/2" (.15 to 1.3 cm) gauge

ENVIRONMENTAL
Up to 25% postindustrial recycled content, recyclable, low VOCs, food safe

TESTS / EXAMINATIONS
Commercial Grade, Class A Fire Rated (NFPA 280) corner room test

LIMITATIONS
Not recommended as permanent flooring

CONTACT
Robin Reigi Inc.
48 West 21st Street
New York, NY 10010
Tel: 212-924-5558
www.robin-reigi.com
info@robin-reigi.com

Workstation 2.0

TRANSLUCENT STRUCTURAL HONEYCOMB DESK

The Panelite Workstation 2.0 was originally designed in 2003 for the Illinois Institute of Technology's McCormick Tribune Campus Center in collaboration with Office for Metropolitan Architecture. The single monolithic panel of 2 inch (5.1 centimeter) thick honeycomb spans 7 feet (2.1 meters) and features a mitered corner opposite a 6 inch (15.2 centimeter) radius corner. Continuous fiberglass-reinforced-resin edging on each side exposes the honeycomb pattern while providing additional structural strength.

The core used in the Panelite cast polymer series panels is produced from 80 percent postconsumer recycled material mainly from recycled PET bottles or high-quality pharmaceutical and food packaging. Panelite supplies Workstation 2.0 in standard resin colors (orange, blue, light blue, green, magenta, red, light honey, and dark honey) and produces the table in custom colors based on a Pantone number or color chip.

CONTENTS
Polymer honeycomb core, fiberglass-reinforced cast-resin facings

APPLICATIONS
Work surface, display table

TYPES / SIZES
30 x 72 x 29" (76.2 x 182.9 x 73.7 cm); standard colors orange, blue, light blue, green, magenta, red, light honey, dark honey; custom color based on a Pantone number or color chip

ENVIRONMENTAL
Panel core made from 80% postconsumer recycled PET

TESTS / EXAMINATIONS
Class C fire-rating for flame spread only (not smoke developed)

LIMITATIONS
Not recommended for exterior use

CONTACT
Panelite
5835 Adams Boulevard
Culver City, CA 90232
Tel: 323-297-0115
www.panelite.us
info@panelite.us

06: **GLASS**

3D Studio Line

MULTIDIMENSIONAL KILN CAST GLASS

With the increased sophistication of glass-fabrication technologies, flatness and clarity have typically been the most sought-after traits in architectural glass. However, glass is increasingly explored as a multidimensional, irregular, and textured material. Enlarging the profile and depth of glass enhances its structural properties in addition to its aesthetic complexity.

Joel Berman Glass Studios' 3D Studio Line consists of a variety of three-dimensional, handcrafted glass panels. Corrugated, Profile, and Trio glass are based on pure geometrical sine-wave and sawtooth profiles. Boards, Bricks, and Sticks represent repeating architectural building blocks. Arrigado and Otto convey sensuous, organic shapes akin to water or crystalline structures.

CONTENTS
100% cast glass

APPLICATIONS
Feature walls, sculpture, door panels, ceilings, windows, skylights

TYPES / SIZES
Clear float glass or low-iron glass; 46 x 85" (116.8 x 215.9 cm), 46 x 98" (116.8 x 248.9 cm), 46 x 108" (116.8 x 274.3 cm), 53 x 108" (134.6 x 274.3 cm), 53 x 116" (134.6 x 294.6 cm), 53 x 120" (134.6 x 304.8 cm); 1/4 to 3/4" (.6 to 1.9 cm) thick

ENVIRONMENTAL
Reuse of waste glass in manufacturing

CONTACT
Joel Berman Glass Studios Ltd.
1.1244 Cartwright Street
Vancouver, BC V6H 3R8
Canada
Tel: 604-684-8332 x233
www.jbermanglass.com
gstone@jbermanglass.com

Activ

SELF-CLEANING GLASS

Pilkington's Activ glass uses the power of the sun to clean itself. Activ is manufactured with the same advanced pyrolytic technology used to produce glass panels for electronic and photovoltaic solar-cell applications. Activ loosens dirt, gradually breaking down organic residue with a special PhotoActiv surface that uses energy from daylight.

When it rains, the water sheets off the surface of the glass, removing dust particles and inorganic dirt so that windows dry without spots and streaks. Under most conditions natural rain is sufficient to keep the window clean, and in dry weather a quick spray with the hose will achieve the same results. Activ has been shown to dramatically reduce the need for window cleaning, providing crisp, clear views.

CONTENTS
Glass with a pyrolytic coating

APPLICATIONS
Commercial and residential windows

TYPES / SIZES
Available thickness from 3/32 to 1/4" (.24 to .64 cm); can also be made into an insulated glazing unit

ENVIRONMENTAL
Reduces the need to clean windows and therefore reduces the need for potentially harmful cleaning products

TESTS / EXAMINATIONS
ASTM C 1376

LIMITATIONS
Not for interior use

CONTACT
Pilkington
811 Madison Avenue
Toledo, OH 43697-0799
Tel: 800-221-0444
www.pilkington.com
building.products@
us.pilkington.com

Advantic

SYNTACTIC FOAM

Advantic is a syntactic foam made by mixing or combining hollow glass microspheres with an epoxy resin. This high-strength composite solves many of the problems associated with other common tooling materials. Cornerstone Research Group (CRG) Industries' proprietary mixing process minimizes the number of microspheres that break during mixing, a common problem in manufacturing syntactic materials. This process enables Advantic to maintain low density with high uniformity and minimum void content.

Because Advantic is lightweight, it reduces wear and tear on machining equipment. It also has low thermal conductivity and specific heat, so it requires little warm-up time and virtually eliminates plug sticking during thermoforming. Advantic is dimensionally stable and will keep its shape over a wide range of temperatures. The material can also be machined using standard carbide-tipped tools in sheet-fed, rotary, or in-line machines for a variety of applications.

Advantic is available in small or large lots of customized material with custom properties. CRG Industries can customize properties such as compressive strength, flexure strength, material density, operational temperature, chemical resistance, electrical properties, thermoconductivity, water absorption, and surface finish.

CONTENTS
Glass microspheres in a resin matrix

APPLICATIONS
Thermoforming, tooling and pattern making, structural core for aerospace components, underwater buoyancy and watercraft applications

TYPES / SIZES
Custom

ENVIRONMENTAL
Environmentally benign

TESTS / EXAMINATIONS
ASTM 695, D570, D792

LIMITATIONS
Machining of the material produces airborne nuisance particles

CONTACT
Cornerstone Research Group Industries
2750 Indian Ripple Road
Dayton, OH 45440
Tel: 937-458-0210 x165
www.crgindustries.com
info@crgindustries.com

Cascade

CAST RESIN AND SILK SANDWICHED BETWEEN GLASS

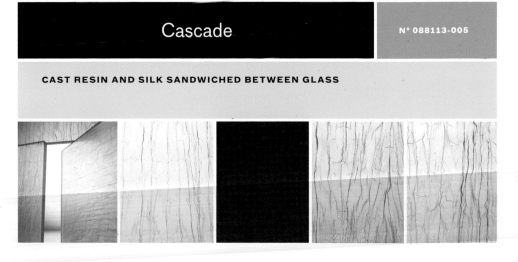

3form Glass is based on a patent-pending liquid-lamination technology that allows for even distribution of objects throughout the glass. It also makes clean, exposed edges a possibility and allows frameless applications.

The newest addition to the 3form Glass line, Cascade, is produced by encapsulating vibrant silk with a poured-cast resin. The result is an intriguing combination of smooth and textured materials; undulating, sculptural fabric is revealed just below a clear surface.

CONTENTS
Glass, poured thermoset resin, encapsulated silk

APPLICATIONS
Interior horizontal surfaces, feature walls

TYPES / SIZES
3 x 4' (.9 x 1.2 m), 3 x 8' (.9 x 2.4 m); 3/4" (1.9 cm) gauge; custom sizes available but limited to 3' (.9 m) widths

TESTS / EXAMINATIONS
Safety Glazing: ANSI Z97.1

LIMITATIONS
No heat forming or cold forming; no exterior applications

CONTACT
3form
2300 West 2300 South
Salt Lake City, UT 84119
Tel: 800-726-0126
www.3-form.com
info@3-form.com

Cast Glass Facades

CAST-GLASS EXTERIOR AND INTERIOR CLADDING SYSTEMS

Shanghai Kang Yu Jie Sen's Cast Glass Facades exhibit superior clarity, have the highest refractive index of any architectural glass, and are suitable for use in interior or exterior applications. Cast Glass Facades are superior to stone in terms of weather resistance, staining, and background radiation. The product can be worked like float glass by bending, tempering, and laminating. The glass can be cast to achieve sharp lines as well as soft organic shapes, and the thickness allows for sophisticated multidimensional effects as well as a variety of color possibilities.

CONTENTS
Soda-lime glass, silica dioxide, lead oxide

APPLICATIONS
Exterior and interior facades, ceilings, floors, stairs, counters, fixtures

TYPES / SIZES
Maximum size 19' x 5' x 6" (5.8 m x 1.5 m x 15 cm); minimum thickness 3/8" (0.95 cm); maximum thickness may increase with reduced length and width

ENVIRONMENTAL
Quartz is a commonly found resource and is easily recycled

LIMITATIONS
Tempering and laminating may not be available in some sizes and configurations

CONTACT
Shanghai Kang Yu Jie Sen
Hua-Xiang Road No. 34
Min Hang District, Shanghai 201105
China
Tel: +86 (21)6-451-8800
www.eastasiaportal.com/luxury
luxury@eastasiaportal.com

Convex Glass

DIMENSIONAL GLASS PANELS

Convex Glass was produced and developed by Nathan Allan Glass Studios with the architectural firms Janson/Goldstein and Front Inc. in New York. Exploiting the potential for enhanced dimensionality in glass, the product is produced in rectangular, square, and circular shapes and allows dimensional viewing from both sides.

Convex Glass can be produced in 1/4-inch (.6 centimeter), 3/8-inch (.95 centimeter), 1/2-inch (1.3 centimeter), 5/8-inch (1.6 centimeter), and 3/4-inch (1.9 centimeter) single-layered panels and can be safety tempered as well. It is available in clear and low-iron glass. Cast textures and privacy coatings are also available. For projects that require laminating, Nathan Allan has developed a new method of casting panels that enables resin laminating to be successfully applied.

Another new process by Nathan Allan is the Fire-Frost opacity coating. Looking similar to sandblasting in appearance, Fire-Frost has a permanent sealed finish that repels grease, dirt, and fingerprints and allows for easy cleaning. Fire-Frost coatings are used in both indoor and outdoor applications and provide extra layers of opacity to the glass.

CONTENTS
Glass

APPLICATIONS
Exterior facades, feature
walls, cladding, wall
coverings

TYPES / SIZES
Maximum size 8' x 12'6"
(2.4 x 3.8 m)

ENVIRONMENTAL
Partially recycled content

TESTS / EXAMINATIONS
Tempered safety and/or
safety laminated

CONTACT
Nathan Allan Glass
Studios Inc.
110-12011 Riverside Way
Richmond, BC V6W 1K6
Canada
Tel: 604-277-8533 x225
www.nathanallan.com
bm@nathanallan.com

Gemstone

SCULPTURAL RECYCLED CAST GLASS

Once glass is tempered, it cannot be cut. If someone attempts to cut tempered glass, the glass will explode. Companies often discard tempered glass when panels are scratched, damaged, or ordered by mistake. Nathan Allan has eliminated the need to discard glass using a process that formulates and detempers the tempered glass. The company makes all of its products from excess glass that it detempers and prepares for a second life.

Gemstone is a cast glass with freeform surface textures. Because the material employs a combination of clear finish colors with pearlescent coating, it is appropriate for applications in which backlighting is difficult. Nathan Allan manufactures Gemstone in fifty-five standard textures and four standard colors, and they are able to match any Pantone color.

CONTENTS
Glass

APPLICATIONS
Feature walls, column cladding

TYPES / SIZES
Four standard colors (translucent colors with frosted finish), 55 standard textures, 8 freeform patterns, custom colors available

ENVIRONMENTAL
Recycled content, abundant resource

LIMITATIONS
One-sided viewing

CONTACT
Nathan Allan Glass Studios Inc.
110-12011 Riverside Way
Richmond, BC V6W 1K6
Canada
Tel: 604-277-8533 x225
www.nathanallan.com
bm@nathanallan.com

IQ Glass

RADIANT-HEATING GLASS

Spaces clad primarily in glass are often poorly insulated and uncomfortably cold during winter months. Condensation is also a problem when single-pane glass encounters a large temperature differential. Although glass technology has improved considerably, the low surface temperature of traditional glass remains a problem.

IQ Glass is an electrically heated glass that addresses the temperature differential at its source. Depending on the local climate conditions and percentage of glass used in the facade, IQ Glass may be used as the sole heating source in a building. According to the manufacturer, IQ Glass will provide heating during the most severe winter months and conversely block solar radiation during the hottest summer months, all while providing a 15 to 35 percent energy savings when compared to traditional systems.

CONTENTS
Electrically heated
insulating glass unit

APPLICATIONS
Commercial, residential,
hospitality, and sports
facilities

TYPES / SIZES
Custom, may be combined
with many other types of
glass

ENVIRONMENTAL
Energy efficiency, 0.14
U-value, 0.48 solar heat
gain coefficient (SHGC)

CONTACT
IQ Glass Inc.
P.O. Box 68713
Nashville, TN 37206
Tel: 888-508-6711
www.iqglass.com
info@iqglass.com

Kiln Glass Textures

TEXTURED, TRANSLUCENT CAST GLASS

Preferred for its ability to deliver transparency and views, glass has typically been appreciated for its ability to nearly disappear; its use in modern commercial applications may be described to be anonymous. Recently, however, glass has been examined and researched for its ability to obscure, refract, and hold light with integrated textures, colors, and shapes. In this way, glass has become increasingly imbued with identity.

Vancouver-based Joel Berman Glass Studios produces kiln-cast glass panels with a variety of textures and surface treatments. Designed for interior and exterior applications, Kiln Glass Textures obscures views while transmitting light through exotic and sophisticated surface patterns. Like board-formed cast-in-place concrete, Kiln Glass Textures carries impressions of other materials; however, the source of the forming materials used in these hand-crafted pieces is not often apparent.

CONTENTS
100% cast glass

APPLICATIONS
Wall panels, sculpture, door panels, ceilings, countertops, windows, skylights, flooring

TYPES / SIZES
Clear float glass or low-iron glass; 53 x 108" (134.6 x 274.3 cm), 53 x 114" (134.6 x 289.6 cm), 64 x 120" (162.6 x 304.8 cm); 1/4 to 3/4" (.6 to 1.9 cm) thick

ENVIRONMENTAL
Reuse of waste glass in manufacturing

CONTACT
Joel Berman Glass Studios Ltd.
1.1244 Cartwright Street
Vancouver, BC V6H 3R8
Canada
Tel: 604-684-8332 x233
www.jbermanglass.com
gstone@jbermanglass.com

LEDS IN TRANSPARENT GLASS PANELS

Conceived by glass artist Ulli Kampelmann, LEDs in Glass was originally developed to expand the opportunities available in her own material palette. Partnering with manufacturer Steve Van Stone, she now fabricates LED-embedded glass panels up to 24 square feet (2.2 square meters) and 2 inches (5.1 centimeters) thick.

Because of the nearly invisible wiring utilized, viewers typically marvel that points of light appear inside the glass with no apparent means of conductivity. These LEDs create low-level ambient light as point sources and also illuminate the edges of glass panels. White and colored LEDs are available, and bulb life is estimated at 20,000 to 40,000 hours.

CONTENTS
Glass, LEDs

APPLICATIONS
Horizontal and vertical
transparent surfaces,
furniture

TYPES / SIZES
White, blue, green, red, and
yellow LEDs; maximum
panel size 4 x 6' (1.2 x 1.8
m), thickness 3/8 to 2"
(.95 to 5.1 cm)

ENVIRONMENTAL
Recyclable

LIMITATIONS
Must use UV-blocking glass
for exterior applications

CONTACT
LEDs in Glass
1150 Drew Street
Clearwater, FL 33755
Tel: 727-442-7132
www.ledsinglass.com
ledsinglass@yahoo.com

RECOMBINANT MATERIAL

Meshglass

STAINED-GLASS AND MIRROR SURFACING

Meshglass is a flexible tiling system comprised of stained-glass and mirror pieces connected to a fiberglass mesh backing. Designed to overlay complex, curvilinear surfaces, Meshglass is fabricated using specially developed software that allows custom patterns to be generated directly via the company's webpage. This software issues specific codes utilized in the manufacturing process based on each unique design.

The glass is hand stained, kiln fired, and cut into an eighth of an inch (.3 centimeter) thick pieces before being adhered to the fiberglass mesh. The glass is UV stable and 100 percent recyclable. Meshglass is appropriate for most horizontal and vertical surfaces, including ceilings, walls, columns, counters, backsplashes, pools, baths, but is not recommended for flooring.

CONTENTS
Stained glass, sheet mirror, fiberglass mesh, 3M fastbond adhesive

APPLICATIONS
Horizontal and vertical surfacing, especially for complex curves

TYPES / SIZES
Interlocking sheets 11 13/16 x 11 13/16" (30 x 30 cm), border trim 11 13/16 x 3 15/16" (30 x 10 cm); weight 1.5 lbs (700 g) per sheet; custom colors and finishes available

ENVIRONMENTAL
100% recyclable, durable, thermal-mass characteristics

LIMITATIONS
Not recommended for floors

CONTACT
Meshglass Ltd.
299 East 10th Street, #5
New York, NY 10009
Tel: 636-486-4410
www.meshglass.com
info@meshglass.com

Mold Gardens

Glass

GLASS SANDBLASTED WITH ENLARGED IMAGES OF MOLD AND GROWTH MEDIUM

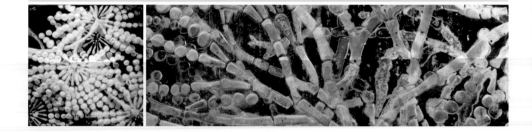

Mold almost always carries a negative connotation. However, landscape artist Stacy Levy celebrates the substance, enlarging its extraordinary floral architecture in a visual exploration that is as educational as it is beautiful. Levy's Mold Gardens consist of enlarged images of common molds sandblasted onto glass plates. The depressions within the glass are then utilized as micro petri dishes, filled with a growth medium and inoculated with mold spores of Aspergillus and Penicillium. The mold grows suspended on the glass, creating a double portrait of the fungus, simultaneously life sized and tremendously magnified.

CONTENTS
Glass, growth medium, hardware

APPLICATIONS
Art installation

TYPES / SIZES
20 x 20 x 3" (50.8 x 50.8 x 7.6 cm)

ENVIRONMENTAL
Visual exploration of the natural world

LIMITATIONS
Maintenance required

CONTACT
Sere Ltd.
576 Upper Georges Valley Road
Spring Mills, PA 16875
Tel: 814-422-8982
www.stacylevy.com
stacylevy@earthlink.net

RECOMBINANT PRODUCT

Stones

RECYCLED CONSTRUCTION-WASTE GLASS

Tempered transparent glass is used in the construction industry for windows and other applications. Construction glass is often over-ordered to account for breakage during shipping and installation. Unused tempered glass from construction and renovation sites that cannot be processed any further often ends up in landfills.

Where the acquisition of tempered glass from construction sites and other postindustrial sources is possible, Joel Berman Glass Studios utilizes this glass in the manufacture of Stones. Approximately 80 percent of a typical sheet of the glass is made from recycled material. Although Stones is primarily a waste product, it appears much more luxurious than the tempered transparent glass from which it came.

CONTENTS
100% cast glass (80% recycled)

APPLICATIONS
Feature walls, sculpture, door panels, ceilings, windows, skylights

TYPES / SIZES
Clear float glass or low-iron glass; 52 x 108" (132.1 x 274.3 cm), 1/2 to 3/4" (1.3 to 1.9 cm) thick

ENVIRONMENTAL
80% recycled tempered glass

CONTACT
Joel Berman Glass Studios Ltd.
1.1244 Cartwright Street
Vancouver, BC V6H 3R8
Canada
Tel: 604-684-8332 x233
www.jbermanglass.com
gstone@jbermanglass.com

Glass

RECOMBINANT MATERIAL

SYNTACTIC FOAM LAMINATE

Synlam is Cornerstone Research Group's family of high-performance, syntactic-core, laminated composites. A unique material design and fabrication process incorporates thin layers of lightweight syntactic composite between carbon fabric layers. The syntactic core is a closed-cell foam consisting of hollow glass microspheres in a thermoset matrix. These spheres are typically 10 to 200 microns in diameter and are available in a variety of materials, including glass, ceramic, and polymers. The combination of this low-density filler with high-temperature, cyanate-ester resin drastically reduces weight while maintaining structural strength and stiffness.

The fabrication technology of Synlam incorporates traditional composite methods and novel lay-up techniques. Specific stiffness of Synlam laminate is significantly greater than that of conventional composites. Coupons of 1/32 inch (.07 centimeter) thickness with .29 oz / in³ (0.5g / cm³) density yielded a flexure modulus of 33 GPa in three-point-bend testing. This is compared with the same thickness of 100 percent carbon-fiber composite, which yielded 21.7 GPa with .72 oz / in³ (1.25 g / cm³). The increased area of surface adhesion between laminate and core layers provides integrity superior to that of conventional sandwich composites.

CONTENTS
Carbon fabric layered with syntactic foam (glass microspheres in a resin matrix)

APPLICATIONS
Architectural materials, aerospace airframes, lightweight mirrors, space structures, instrument housings, sporting goods, shelters

TYPES / SIZES
Custom sizes and thicknesses from several millimeters in size to meter square panels; broad range of reinforcement options available, tailorable to specific application needs

ENVIRONMENTAL
Environmentally benign, not flammable, lightweight

TESTS / EXAMINATIONS
CTE testing, ASTM D3039, ASTM D790

LIMITATIONS
Tensile properties are lower than in conventional composites

CONTACT
Cornerstone Research Group Inc.
2750 Indian Ripple Road
Dayton, OH 45440
Tel: 937-320-1877 x129
www.crgrp.com
info@crgrp.com

Vector Glass

GLASS WITH VECTOR GRAPHICS OF EMBEDDED AIR

Vector Glass combines the the precision of digital fabrication with the serendipity of handmade, kiln-formed glass. PadLAb works with architects and clients to translate vector patterns, drawings, text, and logos into custom-made panels of glass that contain controlled air-bubble imagery. The process begins by digitally incising the desired vector graphic into sheets of glass, which are layered and then fused into a uniform panel, indelibly trapping controlled air bubbles within the glass. The glass panels can be side-lit to highlight the air-bubble images, patterns, and/or text frozen within the glass.

CONTENTS
Glass, embedded air

APPLICATIONS
Custom architectural glass, signage, fine art, lighting

TYPES / SIZES
1/4 to 1/2" (.6 to 1.3 cm) thick; all imagery and text is custom

LIMITATIONS
Recommended for indoor use only

CONTACT
padLAb
612 Moulton Avenue #1
Los Angeles, CA 90031
Tel: 323-383-6777
www.padlab.com
info@padlab.com

VitroHue

100% RECYCLED-GLASS AGGREGATE

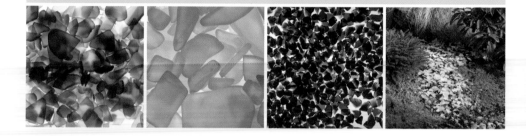

TriVitro's 100 percent recycled-glass aggregates are appropriate for use in terrazzo flooring, tiles, counter tops, concrete pavers, wall finishes, and exposed aggregate surfaces. Available in four colors and five sizes, VitroHue glass aggregates exhibit superior color, luminosity, and quality. TriVitro also makes VitroHue Tumbled Glass from recycled-glass pieces that have been tumbled to achieve an ocean-worn appearance, similar to beach glass or sea glass.

CONTENTS
100% recycled glass

APPLICATIONS
Green roof design, landscaping applications, water features, concrete slabs, terrazzo flooring, counters and tabletops, feature walls, shower surrounds

TYPES / SIZES
Glass Aggregate 00: 1/16" (.15 cm) and down; 0: 1/16 to 1/8" (.15 to .32 cm); 1: 1/8 to 1/4" (.32 to .6 cm); 2: 1/4 to 3/8" (.6 to .95 cm); 3: 3/8 to 1/2" (.95 to 1.3 cm); Tumbled Glass: 3/8 to 1" (.95 to 2.5 cm)

ENVIRONMENTAL
100% recycled content, recyclable

TESTS / EXAMINATIONS
Sized according to NTMA specifications

LIMITATIONS
Not recommended as loose ground cover for pedestrian or vehicle traffic

CONTACT
TriVitro Corporation
18420 68th Avenue South, Suite 101
Kent, WA 98032
Tel: 425-251-8340
www.vitrohue.com
info@trivitro.com

07: PAINT+PAPER

Clay Paint

CLAY PIGMENT PAINT WITH SOY-BASED RESIN

Green Planet Paints offers a clay paint with soy-based resin. Soy replaces the acrylic ingredient used in most conventional paints, which is typically derived from petrochemical sources. Natural mineral and clay-based pigments are added to the soy resin, in addition to titanium dioxide, for odor and pollution absorption.

Clay Paint is offered in both residential and commercial lines. The "boutique" line consists of forty-three colors of flat paint. The commercial line comprises a wider range of colors in matte, satin, and semi-gloss finishes.

CONTENTS
Water, soy resin, marble, clay, titanium dioxide, cellulose, phosphate salt, polymer defoamer, mineral- and clay-based pigments, preservatives

APPLICATIONS
Interior walls and ceilings

TYPES / SIZES
4 ounce (.12 L), 1 gallon (3.8 L), 5 gallons (18.9 L)

ENVIRONMENTAL
Bio-based resin, no synthetic additives, improves indoor environmental quality

LIMITATIONS
Not for exterior use

CONTACT
Green Planet Paints
P.O. Box 13
Patagonia, AZ 85624
Tel: 520-394-2571
www.greenplanet
paints.com
info@greenplanet
paints.com

RECYCLABLE RECYCLED FURNITURE

The value of paper is typically measured by the value of the information it carries; once the information is deemed useless, the paper is discarded. Robert Buss of PUSH> reuses paper in the service of a longer-lasting objective: as furniture.

Disposable Office takes the most common material of workplace communication and transforms it into the workplace itself. Disposable Office furniture is made of recycled paper, with the addition of glass and felt. Individual items are named after various paper functions, such as the Security Documents Chair, Menu Table, or Bank Statements Shelving. According to Buss, Disposable Office is "furniture made from information for the information age."

CONTENTS
Paper with 97% or more recycled content, glass with up to 60% recycled content, felt

APPLICATIONS
Interiors, exhibitions, waiting areas, entrances

TYPES / SIZES
Tables, chairs, stools, benches, desks, shelves; from 17 11/16 x 19 11/16 x 17 11/16" (45 x 50 x 45 cm) to 62 3/16 x 34 5/8 x 11 4/5" (158 x 88 x 30 cm)

ENVIRONMENTAL
100% recyclable, nontoxic materials

LIMITATIONS
Conference chair not suitable for use on carpet

CONTACT
PUSH>
Westerkampstrasse 1O
49082 Snabrück
Germany
Tel: +49 () 541 / 5000656
www.pushdesign.de
info@pushdesign.de

Fragments

PUNCHED-PAPER PLACE MATS

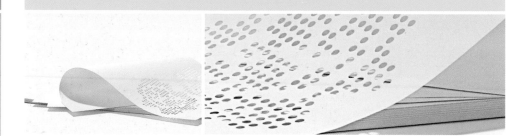

Fragments is a series of paper place mats featuring punched-out patterns. They are all segments of the same pattern design, with references to bindings and punch-card images that form the basis of woven textiles. The place mats are flexible fragments that can be oriented to create an endless number of combinations, and they can be combined as desired to form individual table settings. Fragments actively engages the user in creating continuously new patterns.

CONTENTS
100% paper

APPLICATIONS
Table settings

TYPES / SIZES
Available in white; 13 3/8 x
17 11/16" (34 x 45 cm)

ENVIRONMENTAL
100% recyclable

LIMITATIONS
Disposable

CONTACT
Ane Lykke
Stockholmsgade 53 kld.
2100 Copenhagen
Denmark
Tel: 0045 2425 2849
www.anelykke.com
mind@anelykke.com

Humidifier

PAPER-BASED HUMIDIFIER WITH HYDROPHOBIC COATING

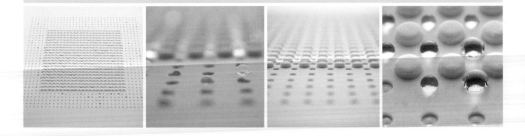

When water droplets fall on lotus leaves, they bead up into balls. Dubbed the "lotus effect," this phenomenon occurs because the infinitesimal hairs coating the surface of the leaves repel water. Super hydrophobic coating is the technology by which the lotus effect is scientifically engineered and was developed for use in special paints and coatings for self-cleaning and snow-repelling surfaces.

Designer Kenya Hara employs this technology in a natural humidifier with no electro-mechanical parts. Daring to use paper as his base material, Hara applied a coating of hydrophobic aerosol developed by NTT Advanced Technology Corporation. Imbued with a surface microstructure similar to that of a lotus leaf, the paper causes most of the water placed on it to turn immediately into round drops. With the transformation of a fixed amount of water into many small balls, the increased surface area accelerates the evaporation of the water and makes apparent the humidifying effect. Because the water need not be heated, the humidifier requires zero energy.

CONTENTS
Paper with super
hydrophobic surface

APPLICATIONS
Art installation,
humidification

ENVIRONMENTAL
No electrical energy or
mechanical parts required

CONTACT
Kenya Hara
1-13-13 Ginza,
Chuo-kuTokyo 104-0061
Japan
Tel: +81 (03) 3567-3524
www.ndc.co.jp/hara

Moss and Lam

MULTIDIMENSIONAL MIXED-MEDIA SURFACES

Moss and Lam is a custom art studio based in Toronto. The firm specializes in the design, development, and installation of custom art for high-profile commercial projects. Moss and Lam uses mixed media to create custom installations offering a particular interest and expertise working in plaster, fabric, leather, glass, paint, and paper. Moss and Lam thus continue to redefine the notion of the modern feature wall based on their background in theatrical and faux finishing.

CONTENTS
Paint, plaster, fabric, paper, leather, glass

APPLICATIONS
Walls, ceilings, drapery panels, volumetric forms

TYPES / SIZES
Custom

ENVIRONMENTAL
Low-VOC paints and finishes

LIMITATIONS
Typically used in higher budget commercial projects

CONTACT
Robin Reigi Inc.
48 West 21st Street
New York, NY 10010
Tel: 212-924-5558
www.robin-reigi.com
info@robin-reigi.com

RECYCLED PAPER AND CASHEW-NUT-SHELL-RESIN BIOCOMPOSITE

Manufactured by KlipTech Composites, PaperStone is comprised of 100 percent postconsumer recycled paper encapsulated within a non-petroleum-based resin binder. The resin is derived entirely from cashew nut shells and is otherwise known as cashew nut shell liquid (CSNL), which has been used for brake linings and drying oil.

PaperStone is roughly 60 percent paper and 40 percent resin by weight and is supplied with a UV-resistant surface coating. The incredibly durable panel is available in 30 inch (76.2 centimeter) or 60 inch (152.4 centimeter) widths and 8 foot (2.4 meter) to 12 foot (3.7 meter) lengths and from 1/4 inch to 2 inches (.6 to 5.1 centimeters) thick. It may be modified with conventional woodworking tools, and panel edges generally do not require protection.

CONTENTS

100% postconsumer recycled paper, cashew-nut-shell resin, UV-protective coating

APPLICATIONS

Exterior or interior vertical or horizontal uses

TYPES / SIZES

Various colors; 30 or 60" (76.2 or 152.4 cm) wide, 8, 10, or 12' (2.4, 3, or 3.7 m) long, 1/4 to 2" (.6 to 5.1 cm) thick; wood veneer optional

ENVIRONMENTAL

Made from 100% recycled paper and nonpetrochemical resin

CONTACT

KlipTech Composites
2999 John Stevens Way
Hoquiam, WA 98550
Tel: 360-538-9815
www.kliptech.com
info@kliptech.com

Printed Food

TWO-DIMENSIONAL INFORMATION-CARRYING FOOD

Printed Food is an edible material that provides a way to convey the nutritious elements of food to consumers in an extremely compact, visually appealing, and information-rich manner. Developed by Chef Homaro Cantu, Printed Food has a number of possible applications, including the delivery of nutritional supplements and ingestible pharmaceuticals, as well as for promotional and advertising uses.

The manufacturing process of Printed Food allows for the incorporation of text and images, such as the food ingredients, directly on digestible food. Instructions for usage, references, and storage information may also be included. Chef Cantu even "serves" a dinner menu as Printed Food. Printed Food's stability, compact nature, and innovative communication capability make it an ideal food source for people in extreme environments, such as outer space or countries with severely limited resources.

CONTENTS
Wide range of edible materials, including pharmaceutical, dental, and nutraceutical ingredients

APPLICATIONS
Informed nutrition, advertising, promotion, famine relief, pharmaceutical, dental, aerospace, identity-theft prevention

TYPES / SIZES
Water, alcohol, or oil soluble

ENVIRONMENTAL
Not made from cellulose composites or harmful chemicals like standard paper

TESTS / EXAMINATIONS
100% certified organic and all-natural

LIMITATIONS
Susceptible to moisture and heat damage outside a controlled (packaged) environment

CONTACT
Homaro Cantu
3829 North Tripp Avenue
Chicago, IL 60641
Tel: 773-580-5930
www.cantudesigns.com
press@cantudesigns.com

Reben

ALL-NATURAL AIR-CLEANING PAINT

Developed by Japan-based Suzuran Corporation, Reben is an environmentally remediating paint made from 100 percent natural ingredients. Created as a response to sick-building syndrome and poor indoor-air quality, Reben emits no harmful volatile organic compounds and actually cleans the air.

The environmentally friendly coating of Reben, which means "alive" in German, is composed of powdered Japanese washi paper, seaweed glue, scallop-shell powder, titanium dioxide, and natural pigments. Washi naturally controls humidity, absorbing moisture during the summer and releasing it during the winter. Scallop-shell powder prevents mold and bacteria growth, as well as flame-spread. Titanium dioxide acts as a photocatalyst, deodorizing the air and absorbing pollution when the paint surface is illuminated.

Despite its completely natural and edible composition, Reben is a durable coating that is preferable to wallpaper. Its textured surface conveys a plasterlike richness, and it is available in a variety of textures, colors, and integrated natural grasses. Reben has no chemical glues or dyes that would negate its positive effects.

CONTENTS
Japanese washi paper, seaweed, scallop-shell powder, titanium dioxide, natural pigments

APPLICATIONS
Interior paint applications in residential, hospitality, and low-impact commercial uses

TYPES / SIZES
Various colors; light and medium textured finish; optional decorative grass

ENVIRONMENTAL
Improves air quality, absorbs odors, controls humidity, prevents mold

LIMITATIONS
High-impact areas require repainting

CONTACT
YDNY Inc.
57 East 11th Street, 3B
New York, NY 10003
Tel: 212-228-0223
www.ydny.com
contact@ydny

Self-Structured Sliding Doors

SELF-SUPPORTING PAPER SCREENS

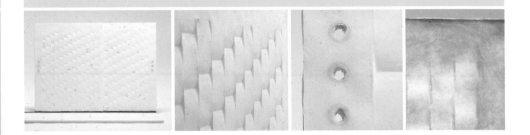

Traditional Japanese shoji are sliding doors made of washi paper supported by wood crosspieces. The paper offers privacy and protection from wind but requires the lattice structure for support. For the Takeo Corporation's Haptic exhibition, Japanese architect and materials researcher Hiroshi Ota set out to rethink the traditional Japanese architectural feature. After researching the Japanese papermaking technique called kami-suki (paper-scooping), Ota hypothesized that it would be possible to make self-supporting paper screens.

Ota formed a stainless-steel screen with a dimensional basket weave–type pattern using a rolling press. He molded two sheets of paper with this screen and attached them together after allowing them to dry. Once paired in this way, the paper sheets formed a truss capable of supporting its own weight and functioning as furniture. Although Japanese washi is typically appreciated for its lightness and delicacy, here Ota has used the paper to create stability and strength in a new sliding door.

CONTENTS
100% washi paper

APPLICATIONS
Door, space divider

TYPES / SIZES
35 7/16 x 27 9/16"
(90 x 70 cm) panels

ENVIRONMENTAL
Does not require wood
structure

LIMITATIONS
Less light transmittance
than traditional shoji

CONTACT
Hiroshi Ota, Center for
Sustainable Urban
Regeneration
University of Tokyo,
7-3-1 Hongo
Bunkyo-ku Tokyo
113-8658
Japan
Tel: +81 (03) 5841-1177
csur.t.u-tokyo.ac.jp
info@csur.t.u-tokyo.ac.jp

EXPANDABLE AND STACKABLE PAPER SEATING

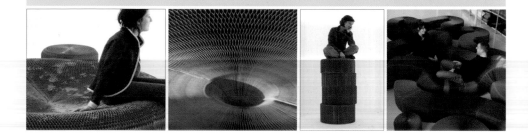

Softseating is made entirely from kraft paper, utilizing a flexible honeycomb structure to fan open into stools, benches, and loungers. Each of the sizes and types of Softseating can be tightly compressed for storage. The seating is available in natural, unbleached brown kraft paper and kraft paper that has been dyed a deep black with bamboo-charcoal ink to emphasize the geometric pattern of light and shadow. Paper Softseating can be used creatively and interchangeably as seating or low tables, and the elements can be stacked playfully as building blocks.

Softseating is not disposable nor meant for short-term use. According to the manufacturer, the paper improves with age, as the surface texture of the paper edges softens with use over time into a pleasing natural patina. When one sits on the paper stools or loungers, the edges of the paper will gently soften and crush, creating irregular facets that catch the light and form a unique organic pattern within the crisp honeycomb geometry of the structure. As the surface of the paper softens, the stools and loungers maintain their structural integrity, because the honeycomb geometry lends the paper strength and enables this economy of material resources. Softseating is flame-retardant treated and 100 percent recyclable.

CONTENTS
Flame-retardant kraft paper, rare-earth magnets, card stock

APPLICATIONS
Seating, tables, pedestals, exhibits, space divider, display surface, podium

TYPES / SIZES
Brown or black; 9" (22.9 cm) tall x 16 / 24" (40.6 / 61 cm) diameter, 12" (30.5 cm) tall x 16 / 24 / 36" (40.6 / 61 / 91.4 cm) diameter, 18" (45.7 cm) tall x 16 / 24 / 36" (40.6 / 61 / 91.4 cm) diameter;

16" (40.6 cm) tall x 7' (2.1 m) diameter lounger in three parts

ENVIRONMENTAL
100% recycled content, low-embodied energy

TESTS / EXAMINATIONS
Flammability Test Procedure for Seating Furniture for use in Public Occupancies under California Technical Bulletin 133

CONTACT
molo design ltd.
1470 Venables Street
Vancouver, BC V5L 2G7
Canada
Tel: 604-696-2501
www.molodesign.com
info@molodesign.com

TRANSFORMATIONAL PRODUCT

Water Pachinko

WATER-BASED GAME WITH HYDROPHOBIC PAPER

For the Takeo Company–sponsored exhibition Haptic, designer Kenya Hara created an alternative version of one of Japan's favorite pastimes. Instead of using electric-light-filled colored boxes and metal balls, Hara employed a simple plane of white paper and water droplets. Paper and water do not necessarily make a great pairing, but once an NTT-provided super-hydrophobic coating is applied, the water beads up on the surface almost like spheres of a solid material.

In a reference to Pachinko and Western pinball games, Hara tilted the white paper panel on an incline and applied white paper pill-like nubs in a pattern. The distinguishing feature of Hara's "game" is that water droplets may either split into multiple spheres or combine with other droplets. As long as the diameter of the droplet does not break 1/8 inches (.3 centimeters), it is tenacious at maintaining its globular shape, but once the diameter exceeds 3/8 inches (1 centimeters), the droplet transforms into an amoebalike creature striving to form a single entity while continually metamorphosing.

Hara has created an intriguing and refreshing new version of Pachinko. While the traditional game numbs the senses with loud noises, bright lights, and conventional ball movements, Water Pachinko awakens the senses with the quiet, unadorned, continuously evolving animation of unpredictable fluid dynamics.

CONTENTS
Paper with super-
hydrophobic surface,
stand, water

APPLICATIONS
Exhibition art

TYPES / SIZES
40 1/2 x 28 11/16"
(103 x 72.8 cm)

LIMITATIONS
Not for outdoor use

CONTACT
Kenya Hara
1-13-13 Ginza, Chuo-ku
Tokyo 104-0061
Japan
Tel: +81 (03) 3567-3524
www.ndc.co.jp/hara

08: FABRIC

Active Protection System

SMART IMPACT-PROTECTION TEXTILE

Dow Corning's Active Protection System is a "smart" textile that remains soft and flexible until it is struck by high-impact force, in which case the material instantly stiffens to help protect against injury. When the collision has passed, the material immediately becomes flexible again.

The active ingredient in the fabric is a dilatant silicone coating, which is a shear thickening fluid (STF). The viscosity of this coating increases with the rate of shear, therefore defining it as a smart material as it responds to changes within its environment.

The Active Protection System is breathable and flexible for outstanding comfort and freedom of movement, and it can be stitched directly into garments, eliminating the need to insert and remove components. It is less bulky than hard armor, allowing for many creative and fashionable design possibilities. The washable fabric can be layered to provide customized levels of protection for specific areas, and it integrates easily into existing manufacturing processes.

Independent testing shows that the Active Protection System exceeds certain European standards' impact protection requirements for sports apparel by as much as 40 percent. The fabric's superior effectiveness is due to its ability to both absorb and distribute impact force, providing protection that is activated earlier and lasts more than twice as long as rigid protective systems.

CONTENTS
Spacer fabric treated with a dilatant silicone coating

APPLICATIONS
Blast protection, sound damping, industrial and geo fabrics, protective garments, sports apparel and accessories

TYPES / SIZES
6'6" (1.9 m) maximum width, 13'8" (50 m) standard roll length

TESTS / EXAMINATIONS
Testing indicates no health or safety issues regarding manufacture or use EN 1621-1:1997 and EN 1621-2:2003 impact protection requirements

LIMITATIONS
No abrasion or puncture resistance

CONTACT
Dow Corning
2200 West Salzburg Road
Midland, MI 48686
Tel: 989-496-7711
www.activeprotection
system.com
activeprotection@
dowcorning.com

BioHarness

SMART FABRIC-BASED BIOTELEMETRY MEASUREMENT DEVICE

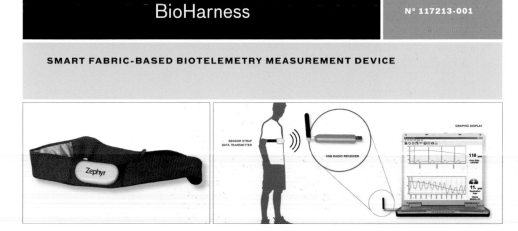

The BioHarness system uses patented smart-fabric technology in a diagnostic tool that measures heart rate and respiratory performance. Because the harness is textile based, it provides increased performance and comfort over traditional equipment. The device is small enough that it does not encumber or change the behavior of the monitored subject, and it can either log a week's worth of activity or provide real-time analysis over its built-in radio link.

The BioHarness software offers an array of real-time and trend-analysis tools. These options allow a coach or medical professional to monitor a subject's performance remotely between sessions. The software tools wirelessly connect to the harness and provide real time graphical display, wireless transmission to 328 feet (100 meters), and detailed records for comparisons and further analysis.

CONTENTS
Smart fabric, wireless radio link, computer, software

APPLICATIONS
Real-time monitoring of vital signs, orientation, direction, and impact for sports, medical ambulatory patient monitoring, and defense applications

TYPES / SIZES
One size fits all

CONTACT
Zephyr Technology
31 Carbine Road
Mt. Wellington
Auckland
New Zealand
Tel: +64 9-574-6523
www.zephyr-technology
.com
info@zephyr-technology
.com

Brush

MODULAR DECORATIVE TILES UTILIZING BRUSH-MAKING TECHNOLOGY

Tactile and whimsical, Brush tiles are ideal as decorative elements in commercial or residential environments. Available in over one hundred colors and fibers, Brush units join perfectly for seamless transition from tile to tile. Brush bristles may be carved for topographical or modular effects, and acrylic substrates offer added translucency, especially when combined with translucent bristles. Custom applications include feature walls, sculptural objects, and furniture accents.

CONTENTS
Natural hair or synthetic
bristles, wood or acrylic
substrate

APPLICATIONS
Feature walls, ceiling tiles,
sculptural objects, table
tops

TYPES / SIZES
12 x 12" (30.5 x 30.5 cm)

TESTS / EXAMINATIONS
Can be fabricated with
Class A fire resistance

LIMITATIONS
Not a flooring material

CONTACT
Robin Reigi Inc.
48 West 21st Street
New York, NY 10010
Tel: 212-924-5558
www.robin-reigi.com
info@robin-reigi.com

Bump

COMPOSITE TEXTURED TEXTILE

Andrea Valentini's Bump material is a sculptural textile made from various fabrics bound to closed-cellular foam. The foam is extremely lightweight and durable, imparting sophisticated Bump-clad bags and furnishings with a notable resilience. Bump is also flame retardant and resistant to ultraviolet light, making it even more durable.

CONTENTS
Closed-cellular foam, fabric

APPLICATIONS
Handbags, cases, furnishings

TYPES / SIZES
24 x 24" (61 x 61 cm), 1/5 to 29/32" (.51 to 2.3 cm) thick

CONTACT
Andrea Valentini Inc.
558 Mineral Spring Avenue,
Studio #106
Pawtucket, RI 02861
Tel: 401-467-7104
www.andreavalentini.com
info@andreavalentini.com

Casula

RITUAL GARMENT WITH LASER-CUT AND METALLIC FABRIC

Italian fashion designer Nanni Strada was invited to design a liturgical robe for Koinè, an International exhibition for church furnishings and religious objects held in Verona, Italy, in April 2005. Strada's Casula became the search for a shape for lyric expression evoking immaterial qualities by means of industrial textile-manufacturing procedures. In a collaboration with scientists from the Conferenza Episcopale Italiana, she devised a ritual garment consisting of two superimposed layers: the outer white garment is decorated using a laser-cutting process, and the internal garment is laminated in light-reflecting gold, green, red, and purple metallic fabrics.

CONTENTS
Fabric

APPLICATIONS
Liturgical ceremonies

TYPES / SIZES
One size fits all

LIMITATIONS
Produced in limited
quantities

CONTACT
Nanni Strada Design Studio
Via Goito 7
20121 Milan
Italy
Tel: +39 02-657-5385
www.nannistrada.it
info@nannistrada.com

Cell

PRESSED WOOL-FELT CARPET

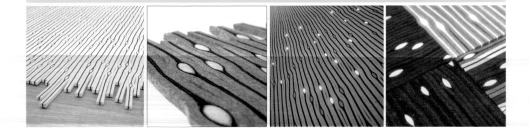

Designers Yvonne Laurysen and Erik Mantel developed Cell while exploring alternative methods of fabricating carpet for LAMA Concept. Unlike conventional carpets, Cell is not produced with a loom, knitting machine, tufting technique, or textile printing. Cell carpet is made of 100 percent industrial wool felt that is pressed and cut into strips. Wool felt is a natural product that is nonflammable, water repellent, breathable, and acoustically absorptive. The size of the carpet is determined by the number of strips used, which are assembled randomly in order to develop a natural pattern with a varied edge.

Cell strips are offered in thirty-two colors, and individual strips may be ordered as replacements. Cell carpet is also offered with integrated LED lights as well as light-reflecting Swarovski stones.

CONTENTS
Wool felt, PVC-coated woven polyester fabric backing

APPLICATIONS
Flooring, wall cladding, acoustic noise reduction, aesthetic applications

TYPES / SIZES
Cell, Cell + LED, Cell + Swarovski; available in 32 colors; 35 7/16 x 35 7/16" (90 x 90 cm) tiles as well as custom sizes

ENVIRONMENTAL
Wool is renewable, recyclable

LIMITATIONS
Not for exterior use

CONTACT
LAMA Concept
Elektronstraat 12, #5
1014 AP Amsterdam,
Noord-Holland
The Netherlands
Tel: +31 20-4121-798
www.lamaconcept.nl
info@lamaconcept.nl

Eclipse Collection

OLEFIN-BASED OUTDOOR UPHOLSTERY

Designtex developed the Eclipse Collection in response to the growing demand for more durable and attractive outdoor fabrics. The upholstery is made using reclaimed fibers of olefin, a byproduct of petroleum refining (destined for incineration). The material is naturally stain resistant, and Teflon is added for water repellency.

Eclipse fabrics are manufactured at a low temperature, requiring less energy to manufacture, and produce no harmful industrial waste. Eclipse textiles are recyclable, and the yarn can be re-extruded up to ten times. Because the fibers possess a high calorific value, incineration produces more usable heat energy.

CONTENTS
100% olefin

APPLICATIONS
Indoor and outdoor
upholstery

TYPES / SIZES
54" wide (137.2 cm)

ENVIRONMENTAL
Repurposed waste material,
nontoxic manufacturing
process, recyclable (up to
ten times)

TESTS / EXAMINATIONS
50,000 double rubs

CONTACT
Designtex
200 Varick Street, 8th Floor
New York, NY 10014
Tel: 800-221-1540
www.designtex.com

Facett

FOAM-ENCAPSULATED FURNITURE WITH DIMENSIONAL FABRIC

Facett is a furniture collection made of foam without any visible structure or feet. The complete encapsulation of foam gives the furniture great flexibility as well as comfort. Designers Ronan & Erwan Bouroullec developed a textured padded cover based on special sewing, pleat, and pattern construction techniques. Available from Ligne Roset, the Facett collection consists of a three-seat sofa, a two-seat sofa, an armchair, footrests, and carpet.

CONTENTS
Wood structure, flexible foam ABS armrests, fabric

APPLICATIONS
Furniture

TYPES / SIZES
Three-seat sofa 74 13/16 x 31 7/8 x 14 3/16 / 31 7/8" (190 x 81 x 36 / 81 cm), two-seat sofa 57 1/16 x 31 7/8 x 14 1/16 / 33 1/16" (145 x 81 x 36 / 84 cm), armchair 34 1/4 x 31 7/8 x 14 1/16 / 33 1/16" (87 x 81 x 36 / 84 cm), large footrest 48 13/16 x 27 15/16 x 12 5/8" (124 x 71 x 32 cm), small footrest 25 5/8 x 27 15/16 x 12 5/8" (65 x 71 x 32 cm), carpet 53 1/8 x 94 1/2" (135 x 240 cm)

CONTACT
Ligne Roset
665 Broadway, Suite 800
New York, NY 10012
Tel: 212-358-9204
www.ligne-roset.com
mail@rosetusa.com

Felt Rocks

RECYCLED-WOOL SCULPTURAL ROCKS

Molo design's Felt Rocks are part discovery, part invention. In their raw form, they are lumps of felt formed as a byproduct in the industrial process of making felt polishing wheels for optical lenses. Small bits of wool fluff gather felt fiber, growing like snowballs as they tumble around in a big drum with the polishing wheels. Each wool fiber is a tiny hollow tube with burred sides. With steam and pressure during the felting process, these little hollow tubes become entangled with each other and form a strong bond without glues or binders. Like rocks formed by the tumbling action of a river, each piece takes on a unique shape. The pieces are selected, processed, and finished through to the final product.

CONTENTS
100% wool felt

APPLICATIONS
Sculptures, toys, center piece, imagination instigator

TYPES / SIZES
Dyed or nondyed; white, moss green, charcoal gray; 4 to 6" (10.2 to 15.2 cm) across

ENVIRONMENTAL
Made from 100% recycled postindustrial material

LIMITATIONS
Hand wash only, lay out to dry

CONTACT
molo design ltd.
1470 Venables Street
Vancouver, BC V5L 2G7
Canada
Tel: 604-696-2501
www.molodesign.com
info@molodesign.com

Fiber Optic Rug

HAND-TUFTED WOOL RUG WITH FIBER OPTICS

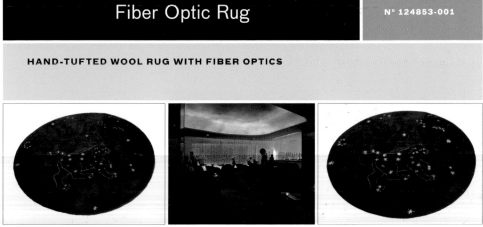

Influenced by an apprenticeship in Japan, designer Jody Harrow developed Groundplans, a floor covering collection consisting of hand-tufted wool rugs with integrated fiber optics. Her Celestial Night rug features Ursa Major and its surrounding constellations, and the stars are encrusted with fiber-optic strands that shine against the backdrop of the dark wool.

CONTENTS
Wool yarns; fiber-optic, latex-backed cotton

APPLICATIONS
Residential and hospitality flooring

TYPES / SIZES
Custom

ENVIRONMENTAL
Recyclable

LIMITATIONS
Not for exterior use

CONTACT
Jody Harrow
136 East 56th Street
New York, NY 10022
Tel: 212-888-9366
www.groundplans.com
info@groundplans.com

Fiber Wall

BIODEGRADABLE-FIBER SPACE DIVIDER

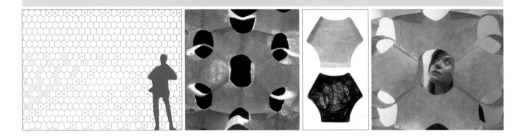

Designer John Hoiby characterizes green composites as fully biodegradable and consisting of plant fiber and plant-based resin. Developed as a collaborative thesis between the Department of Architecture and Department of Textile and Apparel at Cornell University, Fiber Wall was designed to combine properties such as high structural stiffness, light transmittance, and the appearance of natural fiber. It its final form, Fiber Wall functions as a self-bearing, translucent space divider.

Fiber Wall consists of three shapes of double-curved panels. The variation in shapes are kept to a minimum because the hot-pressing manufacturing process requires a different aluminum mold for every unique shape. The composite panels of are made from sisal fiber, linen textile, and soy-protein resin and have a combinatorial logic that allows for growth in multiple directions. Circular cutouts create multiple possibilities in transparency and light filtering.

CONTENTS
Sisal fiber, linen textile, and soy-protein resin, aluminum rivets

APPLICATIONS
Space divider, luminous wall

TYPES / SIZES
Custom

ENVIRONMENTAL
100% biodegradable, annually renewable materials

LIMITATIONS
Not for exterior use

CONTACT
John Christer Hoiby
Waldermarshage 6
0175 Oslo
Norway
www.biomaterialism.com
info@biomaterialism.com

Furore

FLEXIBLE SYNTHETIC-FUR FABRIC

Furore is a porous, synthetic-fur fabric inspired by expanded metal technology. Designers Yvonne Laurysen and Erik Mantel developed the product for LAMA Concept using a special cutting technique. Furore is soft, light, and very flexible and is available in long- and short-hair formats as well as in various colors. The Interior collection includes plaids, bedspreads, and cushions, while the Fashion collection includes scarves, hats, and hair bands.

CONTENTS
70% acrylic, 30% cotton
(top); 100% wool (backing)

APPLICATIONS
Bedspreads, plaids,
cushions, acoustic noise
reduction, apparel,
aesthetic applications

TYPES / SIZES
Long- and short-hair types,
eight colors, custom-made
sizes and colors

ENVIRONMENTAL
Efficient use of material

LIMITATIONS
No washing

CONTACT
LAMA Concept
Elektronstraat 12, #5
1014 AP Amsterdam,
Noord-Holland
The Netherlands
Tel: +31 20-4121-798
www.lamaconcept.nl
info@lamaconcept.nl

Gore Tenara KT

3D MOLDABLE PTFE FABRIC

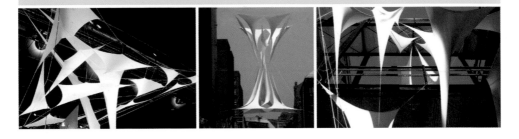

Gore Tenara KT is a three-dimensional moldable fabric made from 100 percent knitted polytetrafluoroethylene (PTFE). Developed in a collaboration with fabric artist Jens J. Meyer and the Denkendorf Institute of Textiles and Process Technology, the fabric is immune to UV rays and is weather resistant, elastic, and durable. These qualities provide improvements in durability over polyester-hybrid PTFE, while maintaining the elasticity necessary to create large geometrical installations as seen in Meyer's work.

CONTENTS
100%
polytetrafluoroethylene
(PTFE)

APPLICATIONS
3D fabric solutions for
outdoor use, fabric
sculptures and installations,
lightweight fabric
constructions, fabric design
objects

TYPES / SIZES
Width 6' (1.8 m), .037 lbs / ft
(.18 kg / m)

CONTACT
W. L. Gore & Associates
GmbH
Werk 1
85639 Putzbrunn
Germany
Tel: +49 89-46120
www.gore.com/tenaragore
fibers@wlgore.com

Hammock Chair

FOLDING FABRIC VESSEL AND SUSPENDED KNITTED SEAT

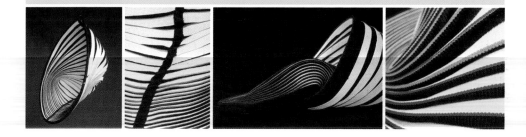

Designer Nicola Lagan conceived of the Hammock Chair as a means of displaying her Mar(ca) geo-metric textile research. Her use of specific materials and knit structures resulted in a sculptural fab-ric with folding, concertinalike properties. The folding property of this fabric is highlighted and exaggerated by use of contrasting colors. Created in collaboration with product designer Tom Price, the chair be either be used to sit and relax in, or be folded into a hemispherical shape for use as a storage vessel.

CONTENTS
Recycled paper-pulp cord, polypropylene, aluminum hoop

APPLICATIONS
Vessel for storage, chair

TYPES / SIZES
Custom

ENVIRONMENTAL
Some recycled content

CONTACT
Nicola Lagan
39 Maskelyne Close
London SW11 4AA
United Kingdom
Tel: +44 (0)207-585-1790
www.lagan-design.com

Ingeo

PLA TEXTILES

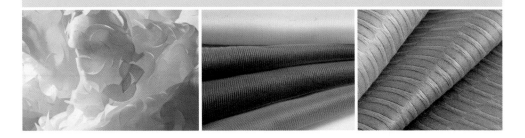

In a notable departure from petroleum-based textiles, Ingeo derives its fiber from corn, an annually renewable resource. Bacterial fermentation is used to convert corn from a starch to a sugar and then to polylactic acid, which in turn is processed like most thermoplastics into fiber. Ingeo is a closed-loop sustainable product: the natural origins of the polymer allow it to be safely biodegraded at the end of its useful life. Future plans include the utilization of corn husks and other parts of the plant that are inedible (known as biomass).

A nonwoven, perforated version called Die-cut Ingeo was introduced with Material Matters, the third collection of textiles to come from an ongoing relationship with the Solomon R. Guggenheim Foundation.

CONTENTS
100% polylactic acid (PLA)

APPLICATIONS
Drapery

TYPES / SIZES
127" (322.6 m) wide

ENVIRONMENTAL
Renewable resource,
closed-loop product
(biodegradable)

LIMITATIONS
Susceptible to melting
when exposed to high heat

CONTACT
Designtex
200 Varick Street, 8th Floor
New York, NY 10014
Tel: 800-221-1540
www.designtex.com

TEXTILE BRICKS

Les Tuiles is a system of textile bricks designed by Ronan & Erwan Bouroullec for Kvadrat. Les Tuiles was conceived as a "immersive quilt" that erodes the fixed character of common spatial delineators like walls, doors, and passageways. The soft textile bricks form a continuous surface that may be easily reconfigured based on contextual needs. Each unit is a "fabric sandwich" containing a soft and acoustically absorptive layer of cellular foam and only requires twenty seconds to be machine molded. Doors are conceived as self-supporting and mobile modules that can be easily moved. Areas enclosed by Les Tuiles acquire a special sound quality defined by a muffled, protected, and introverted sensation.

CONTENTS
Compressed fabric and foam

APPLICATIONS
Flexible wall system, sound absorption, feature wall

TYPES / SIZES
19 11/16 x 11" (50 x 28 cm)

CONTACT
Kvadrat A/S
Lundbergsvej 10
DK-8400 Ebeltoft
Denmark
Tel: +45 8953-1866
www.kvadrat.dk
kvadrat@kvadrat.dk

INTELLIGENT PRODUCT

Recycled Leather

UPHOLSTERY AND TILE MATERIAL MADE OF RECYCLED LEATHER

Spinneybeck's Recycled Leather is taken from shoe-sole scraps, ground up and mixed with a water-based adhesive that acts as a binder. The resulting compound is used as the backer for the Spinneybeck leather tiles. These tiles can be used in a wide range of vertical and upholstery applications and are available in a variety of colors and shapes. Unlike traditional leather tiles that offer little or no resistance to abrasion, fading, and staining, Spinneybeck leather tiles receive a light application of a water-repellent finish, which is absorbed into the tiles and becomes an integral part of the leather surface.

CONTENTS
100% postindustrial and
100% postconsumer
recycled leather

APPLICATIONS
Upholstery and vertical
specifications

TYPES / SIZES
16 ft² (1.5 m²) pieces and
two color ways

ENVIRONMENTAL
Zero waste

TESTS / EXAMINATIONS
GreenGuard approved

LIMITATIONS
Not appropriate for flooring

CONTACT
Spinneybeck
252 Harbor Street
Branford, CT 06405
Tel: 203-481-6566
www.spinneybeck.com
sales@spinneybeck.com

Slinky Stool

Fabric

ADJUSTABLE STOOL CONSTRUCTED OF COMPRESSIBLE KNITTED FABRIC

ULTRAPERFORMING PRODUCT

The Slinky Stool represents an exploration of the structural properties of knitted fabric. Designers Nicola Lagan and Tom Price developed a three-dimensional polypropylene yarn construction that expands and contracts freely, suggesting the form and use of an adjustable stool with its cylindrical shape and vertical orientation and movement. Lagan's choice of color accentuates the contours of the fabric, highlighting the structural depth of the surface. An integrated aluminum knob adjusts seat height by activating a hydraulic pump concealed within. The knitted polypropylene yarn is stain-resistant and repels moisture.

CONTENTS
Wool, elasticized polyester
and polypropylene, shim
steel, foam

APPLICATIONS
Seating

TYPES / SIZES
Diameter 13 3/8" (34 cm),
height 20 1/16 to 28"
(51 to 71 cm)

LIMITATIONS
Interior use only

CONTACT
Nicola Lagan
25 Hampton Park
Belfast, Co Down BT7 3JN
Northern Ireland
nicolalagan@hotmail.com

Soft House

DIGITALLY FABRICATED HOUSING WITH ENERGY-HARVESTING AND LIGHT-DISTRIBUTING CURTAINS

Soft House by KVA MATx transforms the household curtain into a set of energy-harvesting and light-emitting textiles that adapt to the changing space needs of homeowners and that generate up to 16 kilowatt-hours of electricity—more than half of the daily power needs of an average household in the United States.

KVA MATx's designs for plastic photovoltaics, natural photo-luminescent pigments, and light-emitting semiconductor technologies are integrated into Soft House curtains, which convert sunlight into energy throughout the day, shade the house in summer, and create an insulating air layer in winter. These energy-efficient semiconductor technologies shift the boundaries between traditional walls and utilities to create a distributed energy network that is literally soft—a flexible network made of multiple, adaptable, and cooperative light-emitting textiles that can be touched, held, and used by homeowners according to their needs.

Parametric design software developed for the Soft House project guides the relationship of building form to site and allows the energy-harvesting textiles to be customized by design according to the homeowner's budget and energy needs without losing the economic benefits of mass-manufactured production.

CONTENTS

3D knit FR-coated polymer Svennson fabric with woven aluminum inserts, integrated printed photovoltaic cells and smart switching network, Li-ion rechargeable batteries

APPLICATIONS

Climate control, energy harvesting and distribution; space division and privacy

TYPES / SIZES

Maximum width 4' (1.2 m), maximum length 49'3" (15 m)

ENVIRONMENTAL

Energy generation, heating- and cooling-load reduction

TESTS / EXAMINATIONS

Can be manufactured to meet Class A fire-retardant standards and meet NEC regulations for low voltage distribution

LIMITATIONS

Interior use only; not to be exposed to rain or submerged in water

CONTACT

KVA MATx
10 Farnham Street
Boston, MA 02119
Tel: 617-442-0800
www.kvarch.net
info@kvarch.net

FLEXIBLE SHELF MADE FROM INDUSTRIAL-GRADE FELT

Typical shelving systems retain the same configuration when fully utilized or when empty. Developed by Lateral Architecture, Soft Shelf adapts and changes with its contents and can be expanded or compressed to fit a variety of spaces. The basic shelf unit is composed of two strips of industrial-grade felt, segmented vertically and stitched at intervals to create pockets. Units connect to each other by Velcro, and shelf segments can be added as desired. Segments have aluminum eyelets at the top and are hung from a stainless-steel rod like a curtain. Soft Shelf can be hung against a wall or from the ceiling to act as a screen.

CONTENTS

Industrial wool felt, nylon stitching, Velcro hook and loop fasteners, aluminum eyelets

APPLICATIONS

Flexible storage

TYPES / SIZES

36" (90 cm) high, 6" (15.2 cm) deep segments; expandable and customizable

ENVIRONMENTAL

Industrial felt is made from approximately 85% factory-excess wool and 15% mixed fibers; wool felt is a renewable, recycled fiber and is highly durable

LIMITATIONS

Each shelf segment can withstand a weight of 20 lbs (9.1 kg).

CONTACT

Lateral Architecture
75 Kenneth Avenue, #2
Toronto, ON M6P 1J2
Canada
Tel: 416-762 6007
www.lateralarch.com
lsheppard@lateralarch.com

Sonic Fabric

AUDIBLE UPHOLSTERY WOVEN OF RECYCLED CASSETTE TAPE

Artist Alyce Santoro invented Sonic Fabric after being inspired by Tibetan prayer flags inscribed with wind-activated blessings as well as by the use of small strands of cassette tape as wind indicators, or "tell tails," on sailboats. Sonic Fabric is constructed from 49 percent recycled audio tape that carries specially prerecorded audio information.

Sonic Fabric is produced by Designtex in partnership with the Solomon R. Guggenheim Foundation. Future possible applications include fabric that will "speak" its ingredients and recycling instructions in the absence of a printed label.

CONTENTS
49% recycled audio tape
(postindustrial recycled
polyester), 51% polyester

APPLICATIONS
Residential upholstery,
drapery

TYPES / SIZES
5' (1.5 m) wide, sold by
the yard

ENVIRONMENTAL
Recycled discarded audio
tapes, recycling information
may be recorded onto
the tape

TESTS / EXAMINATIONS
80,000 double rubs

LIMITATIONS
Tape head must be
moved at a uniform rate
to understand audio

CONTACT
Designtex
200 Varick Street, 8th Floor
New York, NY 10014
Tel: 800-221-1540
www.designtex.com

HIGH-PERFORMANCE ACOUSTICAL PANEL AND WALLCOVERING

Texaa manufacturers a suite of products, including Strato, Stereo, and Vibrasto panels, engineered to address the acoustical challenges of any room. Strato and Stereo are rigid sound-absorbing panels also faced with Texaa's acoustic knit fabric, Aeria. Easy to clean and install, Stereo panels are available in single units of 2 x 4 feet (.6 x 1.2 meters), 4 x 4 feet (1.2 x 1.2 meters), and 4 x 8 feet (1.2 x 2.4 meters). Strato is available in groupings of four or more interlocking panels and has been developed specifically for ceiling applications. Stereo is ideal for ceilings or walls. Both products are framed in lightweight aluminum with all attachments and accessories available within the Texaa system. The implementation of Strato or Stereo panels on 30 to 40 percent of the ceiling surface is typically sufficient for sound absorption.

Vibrasto is a soft to the touch yet highly durable, lightfast, and flame-retardant acoustical wallcovering. Ideal for large- and medium-scale commercial applications, it is available in roll goods up to 59 inches (149.9 centimeters) wide and 40 inches (101.6 centimeters) long and in 23 colors. Vibrasto offers wide spans of color with minimal seams and superior acoustical performance on flat or curved walls and ceilings. Comprised of a high-performance, acoustically transparent knit facing bonded to a sound-absorbing-foam backer, Vibrasto is available in 3/16, 3/8, and 3/4 inch (.5, 1, and 2 centimeter) thicknesses. The pencil-line detail using factory-provided U channeling allows for precise panel-to-panel transitions. Texaa provides adhesive and finishing tools for installation.

CONTENTS
Polyvinyl fabric, urethane foams

APPLICATIONS
Sound absorption in walls and ceilings

TYPES / SIZES
Vibrasto comes as a roll 59" (149.9 cm) wide up to 40" (12.2 m) long; Stereo and Strato are modular panels available as 2 x 4' (.6 x 1.2 m), 4 x 4' (1.2 x 1.2 m), and 4 x 8' (1.2 x 2.4 m), all 2" (5.1 cm) thick with three different kinds of edges

TESTS / EXAMINATIONS
ASTM E 84 Class 1, NRC 1, water repellence AATCC118 (scale 1 to 6): 5, light fastness ISO 105-B02, abrasion resistance (530-nb rubs)

CONTACT
Robin Reigi Inc.
48 West 21st Street
New York, NY 10010
Tel: 212-924-5558
www.robin-reigi.com
info@robin-reigi.com

Vectran

HIGH-PERFORMANCE LCP YARN

Vectran is a high-performance multifilament yarn spun from liquid crystal polymer (LCP). Vectran fiber exhibits exceptional strength and rigidity and is five times stronger than steel and ten times stronger than aluminum by weight. The fiber's positive characteristics include high abrasion resistance, excellent flexibility, minimal moisture absorption, excellent chemical resistance, low coefficient of thermal expansion, and high impact resistance.

LCP polymer molecules are stiff, rodlike structures organized in ordered domains in the solid and fluid states. Vectran fiber is formed by melt-extrusion of the LCP through fine diameter capillaries, during which the molecular domains orient parallel to the fiber axis. Based on their superior microstructure, Vectran fibers are used in high-demand applications where other materials fail to perform, including aerospace, ocean exploration and development, electronic-support structures, recreation and leisure industries, safety materials, industrial applications, ropes and cables, composites, protective apparel, and high-pressure inflatables.

CONTENTS
Liquid crystal polymer (LCP) fiber

APPLICATIONS
Aerospace, marine exploration, electronic support, recreation and leisure, industrial applications, ropes and cables, composites, protective clothing, high-pressure inflatables

TYPES / SIZES
Vectran NT, HT, UM

ENVIRONMENTAL
Low off-gassing

CONTACT
Kuraray America Inc.
460-E Greenway Industrial Drive
Fort Mill, SC 29708
Tel: 803-396-7351
www.vectran.net

Veritex

HIGH-STRAIN-FABRIC SHAPE-MEMORY COMPOSITE

RECOMBINANT MATERIAL

Shape-memory composites are made with resins whose qualities have been altered to give them dynamic properties. Under thermal stimuli, shape-memory polymers exhibit a radical change from a rigid polymer to a very elastic state then back to a rigid state again.

Veritex is similar to other high-performance composites, except that it uses a high-strain fabric with Veriflex shape-memory resin as the matrix. Fabrication with Veriflex allows easy manipulation of the composite above the activation temperature and high strength and stiffness at lower temperatures. Veritex capitalizes on the ability of Veriflex resin to quickly soften and harden repeatedly. When heated above its activation temperature, Veritex becomes pliable and can easily be reformed into various shapes. When cooled and restrained in its new shape, Veritex regains its structural stiffness and keeps its new shape. If reheated again, Veritex will return to its original memory shape.

CONTENTS
High-strain fabric, shape-memory polystyrene matrix

APPLICATIONS
Deployable temporary housing, dynamic structures and habitats, automotive components, adaptive reinforcement, trapped tooling

TYPES / SIZES
3-ply and 6 ply thickness; 4 x 6" (10.2 x 15.2 cm), 12 x 12" (30.5 x 30.5 cm), 3 x 7' (0.9 x 2.1 m)

ENVIRONMENTAL
Reusability, efficient use of space and material, environmentally benign

TESTS / EXAMINATIONS
ASTM D638, D790, D695, D696

CONTACT
Cornerstone Research Group Industries
2750 Indian Ripple Road
Dayton, OH 45440
Tel: 937-458-0210 x165
www.crgindustries.com
info@crgindustries.com

Vy & Elle

RECYCLED-VINYL-BILLBOARD BAGS AND ACCESSORIES

Vinyl billboards are used nationwide as temporary banner advertisements and are usually discarded into landfills, where they leach polluting materials. Upset by this wasteful practice, Nicola Freegard and Robin Janson founded Vy & Elle in 2002 in order to transform this landfill-bound material into durable and vibrant products.

The strength of PVC vinyl makes it an ideal material for reuse, and the different images printed on the vinyl adds to its visual interest as a fabric. The material offers colorful graphics that take urban art into everyday living, and with its random colors and designs, each bag and accessory item Vy & Elle makes is unique. Vy & Elle is also developing wall coverings, furniture, temporary shelter, and tarp applications with the recycled vinyl.

Vy & Elle is currently working with the billboard industry to develop more environmentally sensitive PVC applications as well as the eventual termination of the production of PVC altogether. The company currently recycles 100 percent of their scrap material into garden hosing and flooring.

CONTENTS
Recycled billboard vinyl (shell), nylon (trim and lining)

APPLICATIONS
Bags and accessories, optional wallcovering or temporary shelters

TYPES / SIZES
Over 50 products, sizes vary

ENVIRONMENTAL
Reuse of waste material, recycling of scrap material

LIMITATIONS
Billboard paint application will wear if used on corners or folds

CONTACT
Vy & Elle
299 South Park Avenue
Tucson, AZ 85719
Tel: 520-623-9600
www.vyandelle.com
customerservice@
vyandelle.com

Wave

TEXTILE AND ALUMINUM ACOUSTIC WALL PANELS

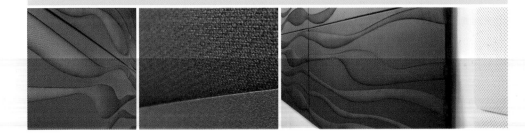

Wave is a system of acoustic wall panels made of fire-retardant foam covered with open structure textiles and pressed into a matte-coated aluminum frame. Creating a acoustic panel more visually arresting than its counterparts, designers Yvonne Laurysen and Erik Mantel cut sweeping, curvilinear forms within aluminum frames that enclose textured fabric panels. The panels are intentionally tillable, creating a seamless graphic pattern when connected. Although the fabric and metal are rendered in the same color, the different finishes express the colors differently depending on the viewing angle.

CONTENTS
Fire-retardant foam, open-structure textiles, aluminum frame

APPLICATIONS
Wall cladding, acoustic noise reduction, aesthetic applications

TYPES / SIZES
47 1/4 x 23 5/8" (120 x 60 cm), custom sizes and colors possible

TESTS / EXAMINATIONS
Not for exterior use

CONTACT
LAMA Concept
Elektronstraat 12, #5
1014 AP Amsterdam,
Noord-Holland
The Netherlands
Tel: +31 20-4121-798
www.lamaconcept.nl
info@lamaconcept.nl

Fabric

RECOMBINANT PRODUCT

Zip

ZIPPABLE MODULAR CARPET SYSTEM

Ronan & Erwan Bouroullec's Zip carpet is a simple system of 78 11/16 x 29 1/2 inch (200 x 75 centimeter) wool felt modules that are connected with a zip fastener. Conceived as both a flexible flooring solution as well as a critique of the traditional surface of the rug, Zip suggests limitless possibilities for user-determined length and color composition.

CONTENTS
Wool felt, zip fastener

APPLICATIONS
Flooring

TYPES / SIZES
Pumpkin, green, sea-blue, brown and gray; 78 11/16 x 29 1/2" (200 x 75 cm)

CONTACT
Vitra
Klünenfeldstrasse 22
CH-4127 Birsfelden
Switzerland
Tel: +41 61-377-0000
www.vitra.com
info@vitra.com

09: LIGHT

3D Display Cube

LED SPATIAL DISPLAY UNIT

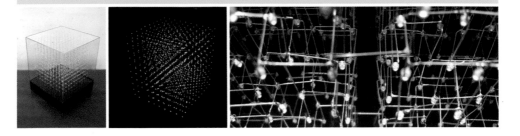

3D Display Cube is a true spatial display unit that utilizes one thousand individually controllable LEDs to create three-dimensional forms and animations. The display cube, with its creative use of LED technology, can be used for retail or public display, signage applications, home display, or advertising.

James Clar conceived of 3D Display Cube as a reaction to the limitations of current display technologies. Televisions and computer monitors, for example, can only deliver two-dimensional information because their display surface is flat. In contrast, 3D Display Cube uses a spatial array of LED pixels, which in aggregate create true spatial images and animations.

3D Display Cube's technology is backed by one issued utility patent and two pending utility patents. Upon purchase, the buyer may select up to five one-minute animations to be preloaded onto the device for immediate use upon delivery. A serial cable is also included, allowing users to design and upload their own animations and content to the cube.

CONTENTS
One thousand LEDs, microcontroller, acrylic casing (no computer required)

APPLICATIONS
Signage, information display, technology-based art

TYPES / SIZES
12 x 12 x 16" (30.5 x 30.5 x 40.6 cm)

TESTS / EXAMINATIONS
RoHS compliant, LEDs burn tested

LIMITATIONS
Outdoor use suitable only for temporary applications (electronics are not waterproof)

CONTACT
James Clar & Associates
8046 North Brothert
Boulevard, Suite 103
Bartlett, TN 38133
Tel: 901-313-4750
www.jamesclar.com
info@jamesclar.com

Burstlight

DECORATIVE WALL LIGHT

Burstlight is light that appears to explode from the wall surface on which it is mounted. Inspired by spiral growth patterns in nature, Burstlight is based on a radial sequence of identical elements crafted with anodized aluminum. These elements generate provocative visual rhythms and intensities when arrayed in combination, and the concealed light source imparts an enigmatic quality to the radiating spines.

Burstlight represents Korban/Flaubert's attempt to explore the idea of a sudden event, such as the moment of a spark, ignition, or explosion. By embodying the spirit of an abrupt release of energy from a point in space, Burstlight adds a visual element of surprise to an interior space.

CONTENTS
Anodized aluminum,
fluorescent light source
(240v)

APPLICATIONS
Illumination, sculptural
installation

TYPES / SIZES
3'4" (1 m) diameter

ENVIRONMENTAL
Low-energy fixture

LIMITATIONS
Interior use only

CONTACT
Korban/Flaubert
8/8-10 Burrows Road
St. Peters
Sydney NSW 2044
Australia
Tel: +61-2-9557-6136
www.korbanflaubert
.com.au
info@korbanflaubert
.com.au

Fiber Optic Room

FIBER OPTIC-WRAPPED ROOM FOR DARK INTERIORS

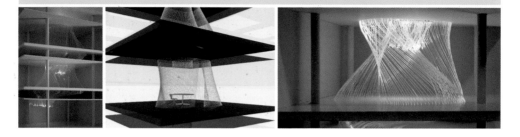

Fiber Optic Room is designed to bring daylight deep into the interior of large office buildings where the absence of natural light is a problem. While this technology is available in a variety of daylight delivery systems, Fiber Optic Room uses this opportunity as way to create new interior space, such as for a conference room or lounge area. Fiber-optic strands are threaded through floors and ceilings to make lofted interior volumes. The strands are either cut at intermediate floor levels to make a chandelier of sorts, or are kept continuous to the floor below. The space between the floor and dropped ceiling is used to make significant changes in shape from floor to floor. At night, the addition of stored solar or other energy illuminates the strands with white or colored light.

CONTENTS
Fiber-optic strands,
photovoltaic panels

APPLICATIONS
Design strategy for office
buildings in areas without
natural light

TYPES / SIZES
Custom

ENVIRONMENTAL
Reduces energy, improves
indoor environmental
quality

CONTACT
IwamotoScott Architecture
777 Florida Street, Suite 308
San Francisco, CA 94110
Tel: 415-864-2868
www.iwamotoscott.com
contact@iwamotoscott.com

TRANSLUCENT ILLUMINATED WALL SYSTEM

Duo-Gard Industries' IllumaWALL integrates programmable LED lighting with aluminum-framed translucent glazing to create illuminated exterior and interior walls, skylights, canopies, signage, and other architectural features. The single-source system can create a variety of programmable effects, such as soft undulating waves, static effects, or pulsating bursts of color.

The custom design-build system may be comprised of translucent polycarbonate or resin glazing panels, framing in a variety of colors, and a programmable LED system with over one million colors. IllumaWALL may also include Nanogel translucent aerogel for high-performance energy efficiency, sound reduction, and light diffusion.

CONTENTS
Translucent multiwall polycarbonate or resin panels, aluminum framing, LEDs, optional Nanogel aerogel

APPLICATIONS
Walls, skylights, canopies, and signage in commercial, institutional, and residential uses

TYPES / SIZES
Custom

ENVIRONMENTAL
Low energy consumption, recyclable materials, diffuse daylighting with aerogel

TESTS / EXAMINATIONS
Fire safety, light-transmittance and weatherability tests available on request

CONTACT
Duo-Gard Industries Inc.
40442 Koppernick Road
Canton, MI 48187
Tel: 734-207-9700
www.duo-gard.com
info@duo-gard.com

Leaf

ADJUSTABLE BICOLOR LED LIGHT

Designed by Yves Béhar for Herman Miller, Leaf is the first LED tabletop light that provides both warm and cool light sources. Leaf's thin profile is derived from a lower blade that can be folded close for subtle, ambient light or raised vertically for wall illumination.

High-intensity LEDs generate significant heat, complicating design and typically requiring a motorized fan for heat dissipation. Leaf's LEDs are cool to the touch due to the use of a patent-pending heat-distribution system, achieved through an engineered heat sink and a stamp-formed, sculptural aluminum blade that allows heat to be released and dispersed.

CONTENTS
67% steel, 20% aluminum, 11% plastic, 2% miscellaneous

APPLICATIONS
Work areas, home environments, ambient lighting or wall illumination

TYPES / SIZES
Available in red, white, black, nickel, and polished aluminum

ENVIRONMENTAL
37% recycled content, 95% recyclable, 60,000–100,000 LED bulb life, low power consumption (40% less than a 13-watt compact fluorescent bulb)

TESTS / EXAMINATIONS
GreenGuard Certified, UL listed, UL Canada listed, CSA certified, Conforms to CE directives

CONTACT
Herman Miller Inc.
855 East Main Avenue
Zeeland, MI 49464
Tel: 888-443-4357
www.hermanmiller.com

Light Clip

PHOTOLUMINESCENT SAFETY-LIGHT FIXTURE

Light Clip is an escape-route indicator that attaches directly to fluorescent bulbs or tube lights as well as their fixtures. Unlike traditional emergency signage, translucent Light Clips are designed to be unobtrusive during daylight hours or in well-lit conditions. This feature complies with S. Lövenstein BV's concept of "hidden safety," which refers to an autonomously operating, mainte-nance-free evacuation guidance system that is only noticed when needed.

At the event of a sudden electrical failure, a track of bright-glowing Light Clips indicates the shortest path to emergency exits, saving valuable evacuation time and minimizing panic. Light Clips are located near light sources, which ensures maximum afterglow. Light Clips are available in various shapes, including arrows, discs, and strips.

CONTENTS
Photoluminescent plastic

APPLICATIONS
Safety evacuation, especially appropriate for public structures

TYPES / SIZES
Various shapes and sizes adaptable to common light fixtures

ENVIRONMENTAL
Maintenance free

TESTS / EXAMINATIONS
DIN 67510

LIMITATIONS
Not to be located near very hot light sources (such as halogen or incandescent lights)

CONTACT
S. Lövenstein BV
Hoofdstraat 45
Terborg
7061 CH Gelderland
The Netherlands
Tel: + 31 (0)315-341967
www.hiddensafety.eu
info@lovenstein.nl

Light-Emitting Roof Tiles

ROOF TILES WITH INTEGRATED LEDS

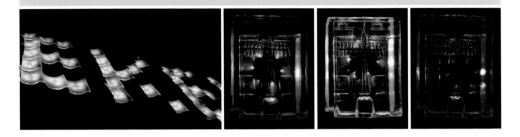

The roof has historically focused on one primary function: keeping out the elements. New technologies, as present in Light-Emitting Roof Tiles, allow the integration of additional functions within roof surfaces. Manufactured by Lambert Kamps, the transparent roof tiles have integrated LEDs and designed to display text, pictures, and other graphical content in multiple colors. Information may also be animated, such as with an illuminated news trailer. Light-Emitting Roof Tiles also come with their own self-supporting solar-photovoltaic power system.

CONTENTS
Cast epoxy, LEDs

APPLICATIONS
Display of electronic
information

TYPES / SIZES
11 4/5 x 7 15/16 x 1 3/5"
(30 x 20 x 4 cm)

ENVIRONMENTAL
Self-supporting solar-
photovoltaic power

LIMITATIONS
Connections are required
between tiles

CONTACT
Lambert Kamps
P.O. Box 1157
9701 BD Groningen
The Netherlands
Tel: +31-50-5731708
www.lambertkamps.com
info@lambertkamps.com

LINEAR TIMEPIECE AND COLOR DISPLAY

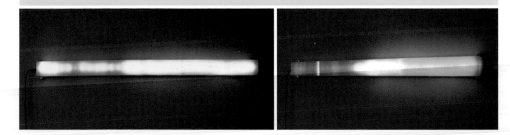

Part light fixture, part timepiece, part art installation, James Clar's Line is a linear information display that utilizes the full-spectrum possibilities of tricolor LEDs. Since Line is a programmable device, it is provided with two factory-preset functions. The first function is a clock, which attributes red, green, and blue LEDs to hours, minutes, and seconds, respectively. Once the time is set using discreet buttons on the unit, the lights associated with hours, minutes, and seconds move through a kind of spectral pendulum, "counting up" to white at 12:00. The second function is a color animation device that displays slowly changing patterns along the linear strip.

CONTENTS
60 tricolor LEDs, acrylic casing, microcontrollers, power supply (100v to 240v)

APPLICATIONS
Clock, information display, art installation

TYPES / SIZES
60 x 6 x 3" (152.4 x 15.2 x 7.6 cm)

TESTS / EXAMINATIONS
RoHS compliant, LEDs burn tested

LIMITATIONS
For indoor use only

CONTACT
James Clar & Associates
8046 North Brothert Boulevard, Suite 103
Bartlett, TN 38133
Tel: 901-313-4750
www.jamesclar.com
info@jamesclar.com

Linelight

LINEAR ILLUMINATION USING POINT-SOURCE LAMPS

Linelight maximizes the illumination potential of artificial lighting by channeling the illumination of one or two light sources along a significant length. Linelight is comprised of a highly reflective aluminum mirror housing with a total reflection of 98 percent, fronted by an acrylic lens designed for even dispersion. The entire assembly is contained within an aluminum frame.

Linelight accepts lamps from 35 to 150 watts in power and will carry light 30 feet (9.1 meters) or more using only one or two lamps. Linelight not only saves energy but also inspires strongly expressive design applications featuring linear illumination. Linelight also simplifies maintenance, as only one or two point-source fixtures require replacement.

CONTENTS
Anodized aluminum
mirrors, aluminum frame,
acrylic lens, lamps

APPLICATIONS
Lighting

TYPES / SIZES
35 to 150 W lamps, 30'
(9.1 m) range

ENVIRONMENTAL
Energy saving, particularly
if used for indirect lighting

CONTACT
Material House
1-19-3, Naka-ikegami
Ota-ku Tokyo 146-0081
Japan
Tel: +81 (03) 3751-5158
www.materialhouse.co.jp
inq@materialhouse.co.jp

Mirror Duct System

HIGH-EFFICIENCY DAYLIGHTING SYSTEM

A significant portion of building construction is made of opaque or light-reducing materials that require artificial lighting. Not only does artificial lighting expend the use of energy and materials, but it also adds to the heating load of structures and requires more cooling during the summer months. Mirror Duct System attempts to solve this problem by extending natural light deep within interior spaces. In contrast to conventional light shelves and larger window openings, which increase daylight but remain relatively shallow and do not eliminate glare, Mirror Duct System thoroughly controls and diffuses light throughout its path into a building. At first glance the system resembles traditional HVAC ductwork, except that it is clad internally with highly reflective aluminum mirrors that extend light as much as sixty feet inside a structure.

Developed by Tokyo-based Material House, Mirror Duct System is a completely passive technology that contributes to CO_2 reduction by decreasing electric-power usage for lighting as well as the additional cooling often required. Natural daylight has been shown to create a more comfortable environment and inhibits mold growth in interior kitchens and bathrooms.

CONTENTS

Anodized aluminum with a total reflection of 98%

APPLICATIONS

Energy-free illumination

ENVIRONMENTAL

Energy load reduction (approximately 65%), decreased CO_2 discharge, improved indoor environmental quality

CONTACT

Material House
1-19-3, Naka-ikegami
Ota-ku Tokyo 146-0081
Japan
Tel: +81 (03) 3751-5158
www.materialhouse.co.jp
inq@materialhouse.co.jp

Noodle

SCULPTURAL PENDANT LIGHT

Noodle is an open, gestural squiggle in space—a loose sketch composed of reflective metal. Manufacturer Korban/Flaubert describes the highly expressive sculptural light fixture as "a reflector gone mad" and "an acrobatic surprise." Noodle traces an undulating path of movement in illuminated stainless steel, much like a projective geometry experiments conducted by mathematician August Möbius. The stainless-steel reflector is highly polished on one side and matte on the other, emphasizing the direction and opposition of surfaces and their paired trajectory through space.

CONTENTS
Stainless-steel reflector,
halogen light source (240v)

APPLICATIONS
Decorative feature lighting

TYPES / SIZES
39 3/8" (100 cm) diameter

ENVIRONMENTAL
100% recyclable

LIMITATIONS
Interior use only

CONTACT
Korban/Flaubert
8/8-10 Burrows Road
St. Peters
Sydney NSW 2044
Australia
Tel: +61.2.9557 6136
www.korbanflaubert
.com.au
info@korbanflaubert.com.au

Portable Light

ENERGY-HARVESTING TEXTILE

Portable Light is an interdisciplinary design and engineering project initiated by KVA MATx to provide decentralized, sustainable lighting and electrical power to more than two billion people. Based on a marriage of low-cost LEDs and flexible textiles, Portable Light is a fully autonomous, off-the-grid light "engine" that provides durable, energy-efficient illumination to foster household economic self-sufficiency, community-based education, and healthcare.

A Portable Light uses 2 watts of power and produces 100 lumens of white light, which is enough for reading or performing local tasks. Units may be grouped together to produce 800 lumens, and charging efficiency is maximized with digital electronics and distributed intelligence. Unlike crystalline silicone (glass)-based PV systems, Portable Light is lightweight and flexible, with no breakable parts. These qualities reduce costs associated with transportation, implementation, and maintenance.

Developed in partnership with indigenous communities in South America, the flexible textile form of Portable Light creates opportunities for use with everyday artifacts and fosters greater levels of acceptance of between different cultures and technologies.

CONTENTS
Flexible solar panels, aluminized nonwoven polyethylene terephthalate (PET), environmentally responsible electronics

APPLICATIONS
Illumination for off-the-grid residential, education, medical, and microscale industrial functions

TYPES / SIZES
Units fold to 12 x 5 x 3/4" (30.5 x 12.7 x 1.9 cm) and expand to various self-supporting forms; designed to integrate with traditional weaving and sewing skills

ENVIRONMENTAL
Renewable infrastructure provides energy-efficient lighting; reduces dependencies on wood and kerosene fuel; increases house-hold autonomy, potential for education, and healthcare efficacy

TESTS / EXAMINATIONS
RoHS compliant electronics, meets European end-of-life vehicle standards

LIMITATIONS
Fully water resistant for outdoor use but cannot be immersed in water; rechargeable Li-ion batteries must be replaced every 3 to 4 years

CONTACT
KVA MATx
10 Farnham Street
Boston, MA 02119
Tel: 617-442-0800
www.kvarch.net
info@kvarch.net

Solaris Glass

FUSED GLASS WITH LED BACKLIGHT

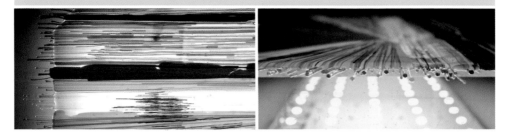

Solaris Glass is a wall-mounted "lightwork" inspired by the beauty of sunlight streaming through stained-glass windows. The result of a collaboration between Los Angeles–based LuzLab and padLAb, Solaris Glass includes a backlight that projects changing colored illumination through a handmade, fused-glass panel. The lighting can be set to run through a default twenty-four-hour color cycle, or it can be fixed using provided controls for hue, saturation, and brightness. Solaris Glass can be repeated in a tiled module in order to cover a large surface.

CONTENTS
Fused glass, LEDs, interactive controller, mounting hardware, universal power supply

APPLICATIONS
Lighting, signage, art installation

TYPES / SIZES
11 x 16" (27.9 x 40.6 cm) tiles, 2,000 lumens / ft^2 (21,520 lumens / m^2); custom sizes available

ENVIRONMENTAL
Low-energy light source

TESTS / EXAMINATIONS
RoHS compliant

LIMITATIONS
Indoor use only

CONTACT
LuzLab
620 Moulton Avenue, Suite 111
Los Angeles, CA 90031
Tel: 323-225-1065
www.luzlab.com
sales@luzlab.com

Square Eclipse

LIGHT-ADDITIVE COLOR SYSTEM

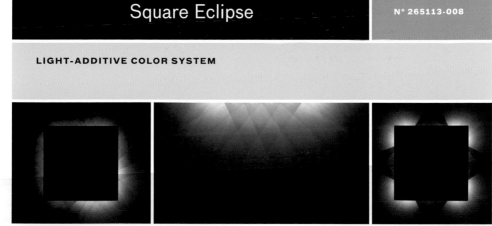

Square Eclipse is an additive-color light fixture that uses twenty-four microcontrolled tricolor LEDs carefully positioned behind the unit to create geometric patterns of light and shadow. Square Eclipse brings attention to its perimeter, creating kaleidoscopic patterns that take advantage of light's additive color properties. The intersection of colored contours from one LED with contours from others creates new patterns and colors emanating across the surface behind the unit.

CONTENTS
24 microcontrolled tricolor LEDs, acrylic cover, 100–2400v wall outlet

APPLICATIONS
Light fixture, art installation

ENVIRONMENTAL
Low-energy light source

TESTS / EXAMINATIONS
RoHS compliant, LEDs burn-tested

LIMITATIONS
For indoor use

CONTACT
James Clar & Associates
8046 North Brothert
Boulevard, Suite 103
Bartlett, TN 38133
Tel: 901-313-4750
www.jamesclar.com
info@jamesclar.com

Textile Softlight

N° 265113-009

SPUN-POLYETHYLENE HONEYCOMB LIGHTS

Molo design's Textile Softlight is an expandable floor lamp made entirely of sheets of spun polyethylene fiber that utilize an expandable honeycomb structure. Light is absorbed and contained within the fixture's layers, giving off a warm inner glow. The facets created within the lamp's honeycomb geometry catch highlights and cast shadows to form a unique pattern. The shape of Softlight creates opportunities for playfulness through the lamp's ability to change. By lightly pushing down on the top of the lamp or by gently compressing or pulling on the circumference of the lamp's base, Softlight's form slightly changes.

The Softlight is available in two sizes, and both sizes compress for storage. Softlight fastens into their expanded shape with a simple magnet connection.

CONTENTS
Spun-polyethylene-fiber
sheets (Tyvek), rare-earth
magnets, cardstock

APPLICATIONS
Lighting

TYPES / SIZES
11 1/2 x 11 1/2" (29.2 x
29.2 cm), 17 1/2 x 17"
(44.5 x 43.2 cm)

ENVIRONMENTAL
100% recyclable body,
low embodied energy

CONTACT
molo design ltd.
1470 Venables Street
Vancouver, BC V5L 2G7
Canada
Tel: 604-696-2501
www.molodesign.com
info@molodesign.com

SOLAR-POWERED-LED LIGHT FIXTURE

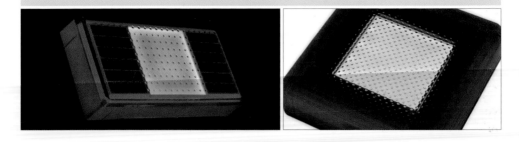

Tsola is a recessed LED unit that uses natural daylight to create energy-free lighting and is suitable for both horizontal and vertical applications. It was conceived by London-based Sutton Vane Associates and is available in two sizes and six standard LED colors.

With the ability to harness energy in both clear and overcast conditions, a waterproof IP68 rating, an operating temperature between –40 and 158°F (–40 to 70°C), and resistance to point and impact load, Tsola can be used in the most demanding of situations and applications. It requires no electrical supply or maintenance and is ideal for retrofitting existing areas where it is unacceptable or impractical to lay new electrical cable. Subsequently, it can be installed by non-electrical-certified personnel. The unit uses a pseudo-capacitor rather than batteries to maximize efficiency and longevity and to facilitate all-weather energy harnessing. It features an automatic cut on-off level at 150 lux as well as high-performance LEDs.

CONTENTS
Single-crystalline solar cell, energy cache, electronic controller, LEDs, polycarbonate

APPLICATIONS
Exterior decorative and guidance lighting

TYPES / SIZES
Green, blue, white, red, white orange and amber; 7 3/4 x 7 3/4 x 2 3/8" (19.8 x 19.8 x 6 cm) or 7 3/4 x 3 7/8 x 2 3/8" (19.8 x 9.9 x 6 cm)

ENVIRONMENTAL
Solar-powered, pollution-free lighting

TESTS / EXAMINATIONS
IP 68 rated, Class 3; CE Marking; ASTM C67, D570

LIMITATIONS
Does not produce a large amount of light

CONTACT
Light Projects Group Ltd.
23 Jacob Street
London SE1 2BG
United Kingdom
Tel: 020 7231 8282
www.lightprojects.co.uk
info@lightprojects.co.uk

Wet Lamp

N° 265113-010

WATER-FILLED GLASS LAMP WITH MANUAL DIMMER

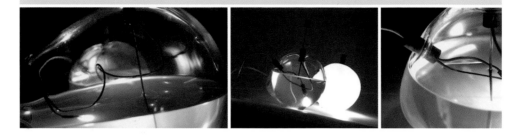

According to Los Angeles–based NONdesigns, water and electricity have become friends. Wet Lamp is an elegant and playful series of hand-blown glass lamps, each with a water-submerged light bulb at its center. This placement of an exposed light bulb in water creates an intriguingly simple dimmer switch: when a thin silver rod is slid into the water through a silicone gasket, the Wet Lamp turns on and becomes progressively brighter as the rod is submerged and delivers greater amounts of current.

Despite its precarious concept, the Wet Lamp is a completely safe product that utilizes low-voltage power and easily replaceable bulbs. The Wet Lamp is approached with caution, but users can't stop playing with it. According to designer Scott Franklin, "my mom always said not to play with electricity near water, but I couldn't resist the allure of testing the preconceptions of such a familiar material."

CONTENTS
Lathe-blown borosilicate glass, 10W xenon bulb, silicone, salt, sterling silver, water

APPLICATIONS
The Wet Lamp casts a soft, moody glow with undulating rings of light that are refracted through the water. Turns on, off, and dims with the simple sliding of a silver rod in and out of the water.

TYPES / SIZES
Clear or frosted finish; 4 x 4 x 4" (10.2 x 10.2 x 10.2 cm), 6.5 x 6 x 6" (16.5 x 15.2 x 15.2 cm), or 8 1/2 x 6 x 6" (21.6 x 15.2 x 15.2 cm)

ENVIRONMENTAL
Low energy use, dimmable function without electronics

LIMITATIONS
Not for outdoor use or water-submerged applications

CONTACT
NONdesigns LLC
620 Moulton Avenue, #112
Los Angeles, CA 90031
Tel: 626-616-0796
www.nondesigns.com
info@nondesigns.com

X-Ray Lamp

LIGHT FIXTURE CLAD IN REPURPOSED X-RAY FILM

Working long hours in the lab, cancer-immunology researcher Jahan Khalili was inspired one night to create light fixtures using x-ray film. Khalili wrapped DNA and proteomic x-ray film around a simple metal wire frame and hung the fixture from the ceiling and created the X-Ray Lamp. The typical lamp is 16 inches (40.6 centimeters) tall by 12 inches (30.5 centimeters) in diameter, weighs 3 pounds (1.4 kilograms), and is comprised of x-ray film, thread, wire, adhesive, and a 120v lamp fitting. According to distributor Realm Dekor, X-Ray Lamp is "perfect décor for those who appreciate the unique graphic quality of everyday surroundings."

CONTENTS
Exposed x-ray film, thread, wire, adhesive, 120V electrical fitting, 16' (4.9 m) cord

APPLICATIONS
Light fixture

TYPES / SIZES
DNA or proteomic films, 16" (40.6 cm) high, 12" (30.5 cm) diameter

ENVIRONMENTAL
Innovative reuse of disposable material

LIMITATIONS
For indoor use only

CONTACT
Realm Dekor
4308 Timber Valley Drive
Columbus, OH 43230
Tel: 614-893-1089
www.realmdekor.com
info@realmdekor.com

10: **DIGITAL**

ARTHUR

AUGMENTED ROUND TABLE FOR ARCHITECTURE AND URBAN PLANNING

Augmented Round Table for ArcHitecture and URban Planning (ARTHUR) is a collaboration environment based on Augmented Reality (AR) technology. Developed by Dr. Wolfgang Broll at the Fraunhofer Institute, ARTHUR augments the exchange of information possible at a conventional conference table with virtual models of houses, cityscapes, or specific architectural components and details. Appropriate 3D objects are projected into the space above the table and viewed through stereoscopic head-mounted semitransparent displays. Geometrically registered to their environment, the objects behave similar to real objects and allow the users to examine them from any location. In contrast to real objects, the virtual objects can easily be modified using intuitive manipulation techniques, such as voice commands, tangible objects on the table, gestures, and gaze-based interaction. In this way, different planning alternatives and proposed modifications become visible immediately, accelerating the overall planning and reviewing process.

ARTHUR can support architects throughout an entire project, from early sketches, to design and review meetings, through to presentations of the final results to clients. The ARTHUR system has already successfully been integrated with the Microstation CAD system (integration with other environments upon request).

CONTENTS
Computer, stereoscopic
displays, software

APPLICATIONS
Support of collaborative
architectural design
meetings, review meetings,
and product presentations

TYPES / SIZES
Customizable depending on
the number of users

ENVIRONMENTAL
Reduction in the number of
downscaled models

CONTACT
Fraunhofer IT
Schloss Birlinghoven
D-53754 Sankt Augustin
Germany
Tel: +49 2241-14-2715
www.fit.fraunhofer.de
info@fit.fraunhofer.de

BACKLIT THREE-DIMENSIONAL RELIEF IN DUPONT CORIAN

Backlight Images are three-dimensional solid-surface topographies created from digital images. Developed and manufactured by the R. D. Wing Company, the Backlight Image process transforms user-provided images into reliefs within the surface of 1/4 inch (.6 centimeter) thick, translucent DuPont Corian. The images are first converted to grayscale mode with 256 shades, and each shade effectively becomes a different height of contour.

Unlike other digitally fabricated products that utilize the relief surface as the viewing surface, Backlight Images are sculpted from the front side. Only when light is transmitted from behind does the image emerge through the material.

Backlight Images may be created from photographs, logos, or other graphic content. Once images are produced, they can be thermoformed to create sculptural objects and curved surfaces. Backlight Images may also be colored using theatrical studio film and can match Kodak PMS or Pantone designated colors.

CONTENTS
Translucent DuPont Corian solid surface

APPLICATIONS
Graphic displays, illuminated wall panels, light fixtures

TYPES / SIZES
1/4" (.6 cm) thick; minimum size 8 x 10" (20.3 x 25.4 cm), maximum size 5 x 10' (1.5 x 3 m); custom shapes and sizes available

CONTACT
Backlight Images Inc.
11809 NE 116th Street
Kirkland, WA 98034
Tel: 877-988-8400
www.blimages.com
info@blimages.com

Bubble Screen

LIQUID-BASED DOT-MATRIX DISPLAY

The Bubble Screen is a dot-matrix display that uses air bubbles as pixels. Developed by Eyal Burstein at Beta Tank, this display can show images, text, and patterns and may be used as a low-resolution screen. The project required two years of development during which experts in the fields of automation, pneumatics, and academia were employed to solve a fluid dynamics challenge. The Bubble Screen is intended to reveal alternative methods of information display and consumption and is exemplary of Beta Tank's ongoing ambient information-design project.

CONTENTS
Acrylic, oil, polyurethane tubing, solenoids, electronic controls, air

APPLICATIONS
Information display, art wall

TYPES / SIZES
Custom

CONTACT
Beta Tank
Adamson Road
London NW3 3HX
United Kingdom
www.beta-tank.com
beta@beta-tank.com

IMMERSIVE VIDEO ENVIRONMENT

Dimension Elevator is an immersive media environment that attempts to demonstrate the fluid transformation of a physical space via seamlessly projected video and audio. Four large rear-projection screens form a 13 x 13 x 9 3/4 foot (4 x 4 x 3 meter) room for up to forty people. Various holistic environments are realized via synchronized video projected onto the four walls and audio played on a four-channel surround-sound system.

The floor-to-ceiling high surfaces provide the images a relative-size context normally absent on traditional video surfaces, such as televisions and monitors—the images are life sized, and the scale is proportional to the viewer. This context is intended to transform the viewer's role from a passive to an active one: the viewer explores the projected content by moving through and investigating the space, in the same way he or she would explore the physical environment.

The Dimension Elevator system can "replay" actual environments recorded using a 360-degree camera or display completely synthetic environments. Utilizing additional sensors or cameras, the room can also be made to react to the occupants.

CONTENTS
Four rear-projection screens with frame, four video projectors, four speakers, computer, software

APPLICATIONS
Information display, education, art installations

TYPES / SIZES
13' 1 1/2" x 13' 1 1/2" x 9' 10" (4 x 4 x 3 m)

LIMITATIONS
Rear-projected video requires large installation space

CONTACT
Dandelion
1906 Barclay #405
Vancouver, BC V6G 1L4
Canada
www.dandelion.org/
dimensionelevator
dimensionelevator@
dandelion.org

INTERFACIAL PRODUCT

Dimple Halftone

TEXTURED IMAGE PANELS

Dimple Halftone is a new process intended to create a microlandscape of texture that, when viewed at different distances, can be recognized as a sharp image or abstract pattern. A reminder of the enlarged halftone canvases of the Pop Art era, Dimple Halftone actually encodes dots into the surfaces of various materials at even larger scales.

Developed by 4-pli and Associated Fabrication, this process allows designers to transfer images or patterns to medium-density fiberboard (MDF) laminate panels, sound-absorbant panels, and solid surface materials like Corian. Designers can simply supply an image with a specified size and resolution for either a one- or two-color surface.

In addition to its imagery and pattern effects, Dimple Halftone can be used to add calibrated performance characteristics to materials, such as nonslip and sound-absorbing surfaces.

CONTENTS
Medium-density fiberboard (MDF), plastic laminate, sound-absorbent foam, wood veneer, recycled newspaper, or Corian

APPLICATIONS
Wall and ceiling paneling, acoustic wall and ceiling paneling, kitchen and bathroom countertop and back splashes

TYPES / SIZES
4 x 8' (1.2 x 2.4 m), 5 x 10' (1.5 x 3 m) panels

ENVIRONMENTAL
100% recycled, low-VOC finishes and glues

LIMITATIONS
Not for exterior use; resolution from one dot per 0.2 to 2.5" (.51 to 6.4 cm)

CONTACT
Associated Fabrication
72 North 15th Street
Brooklyn, NY 11222
Tel: 718-387-4530
www.associated
fabrication.com
info@associated
fabrication.com

Dye-Sublimated Corian

HEAT-BASED IMAGE TRANSFER IN DUPONT CORIAN SOLID SURFACE

Dye-Sublimated Corian is a process by which graphic content, with the aid of computer software, is converted into an ink plate and then transferred onto a sheet of Corian through a heat-and-compression process. Unlike conventional inks, sublimation water-based inks are converted directly from a solid to a gas under heat and pressure, causing them to bond with the solid surface, which becomes porous at 350°F (176.7°C). Upon cooling, Corian reverts to its nonporous state and the ink molecules return to their solid state, permanently transferring the image or graphic onto the surface of the material. The printed Corian can then be repolished and thermoformed in the same way as unprinted material.

Developed by DuPont fabricator Rick Wing of R. D. Wing Company, the dye-sublimation process can produce images up to 30 x 40 inches (76.2 x 101.6 centimeters) without seaming or panelizing. A rapid cycle time allows for fast turnaround for proofing, sampling, and the production of signs, logos, and other design elements.

CONTENTS
Corian

APPLICATIONS
Interior and exterior building surfaces, marine and recreational vehicles

TYPES / SIZES
Maximum single image transfer size 30 x 40" (76.2 x 101.6 cm)

LIMITATIONS
Image transfer requires seaming or panelizing above 30 x 40" (76.2 x 101.6 cm)

CONTACT
Backlight Images Inc.
11809 NE 116th Street
Kirkland, WA 98034
Tel: 877-988-8400
www.blimages.com
info@blimages.com

Erwin Hauer Continua

DIGITALLY FABRICATED MULTIDIMENSIONAL SURFACES

Erwin Hauer Continua is a series of designs for perforated and light-diffusing architectural surfaces. Originally developed in 1950, Continua screens were made of masonry materials painstakingly cast in complex molds. With the advent of current digital fabrication technologies, Continua screens are now easier to fabricate and mass produce, and Erwin Hauer's sensual, multidimensional shapes may now be realized in a variety of materials.

Developed in cooperation with Enrique Rosado, Continua screens are available in CNC-cut medium-density fiberboard (MDF) and stone, as well as precast concrete and high-strength gypsum cement. Panels may be shop-fabricated up to 4 x 8 feet (1.2 x 2.4 meters), and larger sizes must be assembled on site.

CONTENTS
Concrete, high-strength gypsum cement, stone, or MDF

APPLICATIONS
Wall panel, space divider

TYPES / SIZES
Up to 4 x 8' (1.2 x 2.4 m) panel size; larger sizes require on-site assembly

ENVIRONMENTAL
No organic solvents used

LIMITATIONS
Interior use only for MDF and gypsum, MDF not fire rated

CONTACT
EHR Design Associates LLC
55 Church Street, Suite 804
New Haven, CT 06510
Tel: 203-401-8805
www.erwinhauer.com
info@erwinhauer.com

COLOR-CHANGING TEXTILES

Fabcell is a chameleonlike fabric that changes color when conducting an electric charge. Developed by Dr. Akira Wakita's Information Design Laboratory at Keio University in Japan, Fabcell is a flexible, nonemissive fabric made of fibers dyed with liquid-crystal ink and conductive yarns. These materials are connected to electronic components and woven into a square textile. When a low voltage is applied, the temperature of the fabric increases, changing the color of the fabric. When arranged in matrices, Fabcells can display subtle images within the curvature of flexible textiles. Clothing can also be enhanced with temporary self expression.

CONTENTS
Conductive yarns and fibers dyed with liquid-crystal ink, electronic components, controller

APPLICATIONS
Clothing, display surfaces

TYPES / SIZES
Custom

LIMITATIONS
Limited color spectrum

CONTACT
Information Design Laboratory, Keio University Shonin Fujisawa Campus, 5322 Endo Fujisawa, Kanagawa 252-8520 Japan
idl.sfc.keio.ac.jp
wakita@sfc.keio.ac.jp

TRANSFORMATIONAL MATERIAL

Low Rez LED Net

INTERACTIVE DOUBLE-SIDED LED MEDIA NET

Low Rez LED Net is part of a custom-built interactive public art installation consisting of a series of double-sided LED "nets" capable of producing video imagery and animated text. Each net is made up of approximately 8,000 double-sided LED pixels suspended on a cable-net system. The pixels are custom designed, two-sided, and "addressable," meaning that each pixel can be turned on or off individually. The pixel net is therefore a transparent screen, capable of carrying animated text or images with a varying range of pixel pitch.

The Low Rez installation in Washington DC is set at a 2 13/32 inch (6.1 centimeter) pixel pitch, allowing the LED nets to form an image that is legible from a distance while being highly transparent: these nets are enclosed within an acid-etched glass vitrine that allows for translucency while acting as a diffuser for the LEDs. The net streams text and a superimposed live video feed from surveillance cameras, thus inviting user interaction.

CONTENTS
Custom two-sided LED pixel, cable-tensioning structure, acid-etched glass

APPLICATIONS
Media display, interactive art, building signage

TYPES / SIZES
Available in varying size and pixel pitch (resolution)

ENVIRONMENTAL
Low-energy light source

CONTACT
MY Studio
150 Lincoln Street, 3A
Boston, MA 02111
Tel: 617-517-4101
www.mystudio.us
my@mystudio.us

Magink Billboard

DIGITAL-INK OUTDOOR DISPLAY

Magink is the world's first developer and provider of full-color "digital ink" displays. Digital-ink technology is an environmentally friendly alternative to conventional billboards, which utilize bright lights for visibility. Magink delivers full-color, high-resolution, and high-contrast images similar to a traditional paper display, while incorporating the unparalleled flexibility offered by digital media. Based on reflective technology, Magink utilizes ambient light to enhance image visibility and quality—it is a digital display that utilizes "digital ink paste" for programmable flexibility—yet the surface reacts to light like paper.

CONTENTS
Digital-ink display, frame, software-management tool, lighting

APPLICATIONS
Information display

TYPES / SIZES
5'5" x 8'6" (1.6 x 2.6 m), 7'5" x 10'8" (2.3 x 3.3 m), 7'5" x 17'4" (2.3 x 5.3 m); retrofit and custom size options available

ENVIRONMENTAL
Energy and resource efficient

CONTACT
Magink Display Technologies Inc.
P.O. Box 3670
Mevaseret Zion 90805
Israel
Tel: +972 2-533-6007
www.magink.com
info@magink.com

Ombrae System

SCULPTURAL IMAGING WITH OPTICAL TILE

Ombrae System is a patent-pending computer-based image-processing system that allows for any digital image to be embedded directly into any material substrate. The image is not a transfer or material composite, like a hologram, but is made from physical three-dimensional pixels or "optical tiles." The optical-tile pixel creates the necessary amount of light and shadow on the surface of the material to render an image. The material conveys graphic content without lenses, laminate layers, printed dyes, or inks.

This cost-effective surface treatment uses conventional material and manufacturing technologies. Images can be machined into glass, resin, plastics, stone and cast stone, concrete, metal, wood, leather, vinyl, rubber, composites, fabrics, and other materials for uses in architectural settings, industrial and product design, and a myriad of commercial applications.

CONTENTS
Most material substrates, including glass, plastics, stone, concrete, metal, and wood

APPLICATIONS
Architecture and interior design, product design, packaging, signage, and advertising

TYPES / SIZES
Sizes range from coin-sized to large-scale exterior architectural settings

ENVIRONMENTAL
Imaging system operates with natural lighting; no required energy, printed dyes, inks, or chemicals

TESTS / EXAMINATIONS
Based on individual material substrate specifications

CONTACT
QMAAS
#3 1334 Odlum Drive
Vancouver, BC V5L 3M3
Canada
Tel: 604-255-9929
www.qmaas.com
info@qmaas.com

INDIVIDUAL-TRACKING INFORMATION DISPLAY SYSTEM

Radio-frequency identification (RFID) is an automated identification process based on the storage and retrieval of data using transponders or RFID tags. These tags are often associated with objects that may be quickly inventoried, such as product palettes, library materials, or passports.

Keio University researchers have re-envisioned the use of RFID tags with people to develop a new information display system. The resulting Paravision is a dynamic sign system that projects information on a transparent screen. Designed for public spaces, Paravision tracks RFID devices carried by individuals and associates their personal information, stored on a computer or in a network, with their current spatial positions and projects this information onto the transparent screen. Possible applications include interactive exhibitions, automated concierge services, advertising, gaming, and surveillance.

CONTENTS
RFID tags, transparent projection screen, projector, connectors, hardware, software

APPLICATIONS
Interactive displays, museums, exhibitions, automated concierge, retail, advertising, entertainment, gaming, security

CONTACT
Information Design Laboratory, Keio University Shonin Fujisawa Campus, 5322 Endo Fujisawa, Kanagawa 252-8520 Japan
idl.sfc.keio.ac.jp
wakita@sfc.keio.ac.jp

Pileus

INTERNET UMBRELLA

Researchers with Keio University's Okude Laboratory have developed an unlikely platform to showcase content from the burgeoning image website Flickr. Pileus, also known as the Flickr Umbrella, downloads and projects still-image and video content in real time from Flickr or other websites using the umbrella fabric as the projection surface. A simple flick of the wrist rotates the umbrella shaft a couple degrees and advances the images.

The umbrella also comes equipped with a simple camera mounted to the shaft, and a low-resolution photograph may be taken, uploaded to the internet, and actively projected by the umbrella within two to three seconds. Global positioning system (GPS) data is also associated to the umbrella, and a map of the surrounding context may be projected to assist with local navigation.

CONTENTS
Umbrella, camera, Global positioning system (GPS), 3D accelerometer, web API

APPLICATIONS
Information display, navigation, photo documentation, rain protection

TYPES / SIZES
Umbrella 37" (94 cm) diameter, handle 39" (99.1 cm) long

LIMITATIONS
Severe typhoon

CONTACT
Pileus LLC
1-11-5-802, Hiroo
Shibuya-ku
Tokyo 150-0012
Japan
Tel: +81 (50) 5539-8199
www.pileus.net
info@pileus.net

PixelSkin01

SMART FACADE FOR DYNAMIC LIGHT TRANSMITTANCE AND INFORMATION DISPLAY

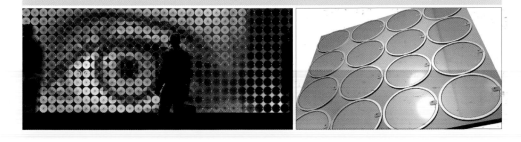

Developed by Sachin Anshuman of Orangevoid, PixelSkin01 is an intelligent cladding system intended to bring information display technology to light-transmitting building facades. Conventional visual communication, such as advertising, obscures light and views for building occupants when applied to the facade and is at odds with the needs of the users. PixelSkin01 attempts to offer a solution via a heterogeneous smart surface that is translucent in its typical state but transforms into either a transparent state or a full-color video screen when desired. The system consists of a combination of electrochromic glass and ultra-bright electroluminescent tubes controlled by a distributed network of microcomputers and sensor consoles.

As a user approaches the surface, integrated sensors turn to transparent the default translucent state of the closest cluster of disks. The diameter of this transparent field is dynamically adjusted according to a variety of environmental parameters. When visual communication is desired—typically after working hours or when a potential customer approaches a retail window, for example—colored light is emitted by RGB electroluminescent tubes at the perimeter of each disk, and each module is treated a pixel within a larger image field.

CONTENTS
Ultra-bright RGB electroluminescent tubes, electrochromic film, microcontroller consoles, environmental sensors, embedded control electronics

APPLICATIONS
Intelligent facades, integrated display and light transmittance, dynamic privacy control

TYPES / SIZES
5 7/8" (15 cm) diameter disks

ENVIRONMENTAL
Low-energy consumption

CONTACT
Orangevoid
66 Osbaldeston Road
London N16 7DR
United Kingdom
Tel: +44 (0)20 7502-2239
www.orangevoid.org.uk
info@orangevoid.org.uk

Recursive Pattern Process

PROCESS GENERATING EVOLVING, NONPERIODIC PATTERNS

Materials produced in modular units based on traditional industrial practices are inevitably confined to predictable, repeating patterns. A common example is the carpet tile, in which repeating patterns emerge despite the frequent desire for an evolving, nonrepetitive effect. StudioStampa is dedicated to changing common perceptions about patterns. The company's design concept is based on creating an evolving, nonperiodic pattern that is in a constant state of permutation, thereby eliminating pattern predictability.

Using nature as their model, StudioStampa generates surface patterns that closely emulate the beauty of constant, ordered change occurring in the physical world. Their recursive patterns are generated by custom-developed software tools, and these patterns are utilized to manipulate a variety of materials for use in interior and exterior applications.

CONTENTS
Digital design based on algorithms used to generate complex patterns

APPLICATIONS
Any two-dimensional surface or substrate

TYPES / SIZES
Vector-based, nonrepeating patterns that are independent of scale and length

ENVIRONMENTAL
Waste reduction

LIMITATIONS
To produce standard collections, patterns are best configured in large units of indiscernible repetition

CONTACT
StudioStampa Inc.
38 Avenue Road, Suite 713
Toronto, ON M5R 2G2
Canada
Tel: 416-515-9658
www.studiostampa
design.com
info@studiostampa
design.com

River Glow

NETWORK OF FLOATING PODS WITH PUBLIC INTERFACE TO WATER QUALITY

Developed by David Benjamin and Soo-in Yang, River Glow is a system of floating pods that monitors water quality and displays a variable light signal that is visible from the water or onshore. Each unit consists of an underwater pH probe, super bright LEDs, uncoated fiber-optic strands, and photovoltaics that provide power to rechargeable batteries. When deployed in public waterways, the system creates an ethereal cloud of light hovering above the water's surface that changes colors according to the condition of the water.

The system is energy self-sufficient, low-cost, modular, and easy to deploy, offering an alternative to expensive and time-consuming testing of water samples in a remote research laboratory. The component system allows for swapping of alternative energy-harvesting devices, water-quality sensors, and low-energy lighting or actuators.

CONTENTS
Photovoltaics, pH meter, low-energy lighting

APPLICATIONS
Deployment in public waterway, in river pool, at fishing spot, or near combined sewer-overflow outlet

TYPES / SIZES
14" (35.6 cm) diameter, 14" (35.6 cm) height, with 4" (10.2 cm) long pH probe at adjustable underwater depth; custom sizes available

ENVIRONMENTAL
Energy self-sufficient, raises awareness of environmental quality

LIMITATIONS
Visibility of signal is limited in direct sunlight

CONTACT
The Living
146 West 29 Street #4RE
New York, NY 10014
www.thelivingnewyork.com

Sensacell

MODULAR INTERACTIVE-SENSOR AND LIGHTING SYSTEM

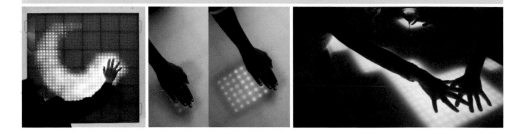

The Sensacell system transforms architectural surfaces into dynamic interactive experiences. Sensacell capacitive proximity sensors detect people and objects on the other side of barriers up to 2 inches (5.1 centimeters) thick, creating a three-dimensional, multitouch sensing zone above the surface. Additionally, the integrated full-color LED lighting array creates stunning interactive graphics, video, and ambient illumination. The plug-and-play system is based on 6 inch (15.2 centimeter) square modules that can be embedded into surfaces of any size or shape, allowing total design flexibility.

Sensacell arrays can be interfaced with other systems to control sound, light, video, HVAC, and alarm systems via RS232, MIDI, DMX, and TCP-IP. The Sensacell Sensa-Tools software allows for the rapid development of customized programs to control various building systems or trigger particular environmental effects.

CONTENTS
Electronics, LEDs, FR4 fiberglass

APPLICATIONS
Retail and entertainment applications, signage, home automation, kiosks, security

TYPES / SIZES
6 in² (15.2 cm²), modular

ENVIRONMENTAL
Energy-saving intelligent building-management systems

TESTS / EXAMINATIONS
UL, FCC, TUV

LIMITATIONS
Cannot sense through metallic or electrically conductive materials

CONTACT
Sensacell Inc.
168 Bedford Avenue, #2
Brooklyn, NY 11211
Tel: 718-782-8696
www.sensacell.com
contact@sensacell.com

INTERACTIVE FLOOR

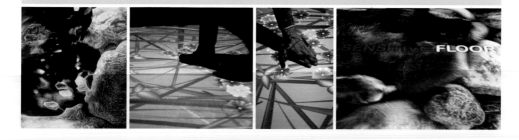

Sensitive Floor is an interactive video floor projection that reacts to the way people walk on it. Developed by iO Agency, this new media for physical spaces transforms mundane floors into arresting communication tools. Sensitive Floor adapts effortlessly to different contexts and needs, such as retail, entertainment, exhibition, or advertising.

Available in a series of versions that are easily adaptable to different situations, Sensitive Floor can be hired for special events or permanently installed in a public building to create a spatially rooted media channel. Because its gamelike interface typically inspires enthusiastic responses, iO Agency dubbed the Sensitive Floor "the first interactive medium that makes you smile."

CONTENTS
Visual administration panel, video and audio hardware, monitoring tools, effects software

APPLICATIONS
Information display, interactive installation

TYPES / SIZES
Minimum ceiling height 9'10" (3 m); designed for easy installation in temporary conditions; floor-projection size depends on ceiling height and projector optics

TESTS / EXAMINATIONS
CE marking and certification

LIMITATIONS
Lighting environment suitable for video projection; availability of a support structure from which to hang the system

CONTACT
iO Agency
Via Cà Zenobio 28/a
31100 Treviso
Italy
Tel: +39 (0)422-435-992
www.ioagency.com
treviso@ioagency.com

SmartFountain

INTERACTIVE WATER FEATURE

A typical fountain or waterscape consumes less water annually than an equal surface area of grass-planted lawn. Water features can also be filled with rainwater and used as backup water storage systems for irrigation and gray water use. With these benefits in mind, Jenna Didier and Oliver Hess develop water features with interactive technologies to encourage more widespread use.

SmartFountain encourages people to engage with water and each other in playful games of call and response. A versatile, integrated software system is programmed to provide either subtle or spectacular water effects that respond to facial expressions, arm movements, or directional movements of visitors around water features.

CONTENTS
Basin, water, pumps, hardware, software

APPLICATIONS
Fountains

TYPES / SIZES
Custom

ENVIRONMENTAL
Less consumption of water than a lawn with the same area, storage-tank options available

LIMITATIONS
Context affects types of interactions possible

CONTACT
Fountainhead
1619 Silver Lake Boulevard
Los Angeles, CA 90026
Tel: 323-913-0915
www.fountainhd.com
sales@fountainhd.com

Super Cilia Skin

SILICONE-BASED INTERACTIVE MEMBRANE

Super Cilia Skin is a tactile and visual system inspired by the beauty of grass blowing in the wind. It consists of an array of computer-controlled actuators (cilia) that are anchored to an elastic membrane. These actuators represent information by changing their physical orientation. The current prototype of Super Cilia Skin, developed by MIT's Tangible Interfaces, functions as an output device capable of visual and tactile expression.

Most existing computational tools rely on visual-output devices. While such devices are invaluable, influential studies in neurophysiology have shown that physical experience creates especially strong neural pathways in the brain. When people participate in tactile/kinesthetic activity, the two hemispheres of the brain are simultaneously engaged. This type of learning experience helps assure that new information will be retained in long-term memory.

The ability of Super Cilia Skin to replay dynamic gestures over time and to communicate remote gestures makes it a potentially valuable tool for education and haptic communication. On an architectural scale, a facade covered with Super Cilia Skin could represent the "wake" of a local wind pattern billowing up and down the surface during the day. As a more general display surface, a floor of Super Cilia Skin could trace movement over one's house or weather patterns over an entire state.

CONTENTS
Nonvolatile methyl silicone (PDMS), felt, hardware, software

APPLICATIONS
Replays and communicates remote dynamic gestures over time, education

TYPES / SIZES
Custom sizes available

ENVIRONMENTAL
Generates small amounts of energy from wind movement, ecologically inert

TESTS / EXAMINATIONS
CHI 2003 paper, ACM 1-58113-630-7/03/0004

LIMITATIONS
Currently only a prototype

CONTACT
Archinode
222 Bushwick Avenue, #4R
Brooklyn, NY 11206
Tel: 617-285-0901
www.archinode.com
order@archinode.com

TileToy

MODULAR ELECTRONIC-GAME PROTOTYPE

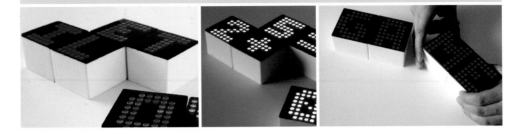

TileToy is a modular, electronic-game prototype for game tiles developed by English game designer Daniel Blackburn with Finnish designer and media artist Tuomo Tammenpää. This game platform brings the flexibility inherent in digital software to a physical tile with which people can touch and interact. By arranging the electronic tiles, players can engage themselves in various kinds of game play, ranging from fast-paced arcade-style games to puzzles and educational games. The reprogrammable and constantly updated graphic information on each tile is displayed with a LED-matrix display. Each tile is controlled individually and can be used to transmit information on its own or in groups of several tiles. The assembled tiles wirelessly transmit their individual positions in relation to one another and a central computer, or a dedicated tile runs different applications based on that information. In TileToy, technology is sealed within the design, and the interaction is based on a tactile experience in which no user manual is needed.

CONTENTS
Plastic case, acrylic,
electronics

APPLICATIONS
Platform for various game
and play applications,
modular screen

TYPES / SIZES
2.4 x 2.4 x 1 3/4"
(6 x 6 x 4.5 cm)

CONTACT
TileToy
Kirkkotie 183 as1
07170 Pornainen
Finland
Tel: +358 40-525-4636
www.tiletoy.org
tuomo@mindworks.fi

COMMUNICATIVE CLOTHING SYSTEM

Researchers at Keio University's Information Design Laboratory developed clothing designed to signal changing individual conditions. Their conceptual model was based on the analog synthesizer, which can generate an infinite variety of original sounds by connecting and tuning three modules, the VCA, VCO, and VCF. Wearable Synthesis, likewise, connects and tunes a variety of "fashion modules" as a means for personal expression and communication.

For example, an inner-wear module that senses body temperature, heart rate, or other biorhythmic condition can change its color accordingly. This information is input via an anatomical sensor and processed by microcontrollers. Once an outer-wear module is connected to the inner-wear module, the outer-wear may generate a signal that corresponds to this data. In the spirit of this coordinated system of information, a variety of accessories, hats, and bags have also been developed as Wearable Synthesis fashion modules.

CONTENTS
Fabric, anatomical sensors, microcontrollers, conductive textiles, lighting devices

APPLICATIONS
Expressive clothing, information display and communication

TYPES / SIZES
Custom

CONTACT
Information Design Laboratory, Keio University Shonin Fujisawa Campus, 5322 Endo Fujisawa, Kanagawa 252-8520 Japan idl.sfc.keio.ac.jp wakita@sfc.keio.ac.jp

White Noise White Light

INTERACTIVE FIBER-OPTIC FIELD

Meejin Yoon's *White Noise White Light* was a temporary interactive light-and-sound installation commissioned and installed for the Athens 2004 Olympics. The project consisted of a field of fiber-optic strands and under-mounted electronics units that responded to the movement of pedestrians through the field by transmitting white light from white LEDs and white noise from speakers below a raised platform.

Just as white light is made of the full spectrum of light, white noise contains an equal amount of every frequency within the range of hearing. Each "stalk unit" possesses its own passive infrared sensor and microprocessor, which use a software differentiation algorithm to determine whether a body is passing by the stalk. If motion is detected, the white LED illumination grows brighter while the white noise increases in volume. Once motion is no longer detected, the microprocessor smoothly decreases the light and fades the sound to silence. The movement of pedestrians creates an afterglow effect in the form of a flickering wake of white light and white noise, trailing and tracing visitors as they cross the field. Depending on the time of day, number of people, and trajectories of movement, the project is constantly choreographed by the cumulative interaction of the public. The field becomes an unpredictable aggregation of movement, light, and sound.

CONTENTS
Custom electronics modules, LEDs, speakers, fiber optics, polycarbonate tubes

APPLICATIONS
Interactive art, outdoor lighting, landscape

TYPES / SIZES
Available in varying size

ENVIRONMENTAL
Uses low-energy LEDs

TESTS / EXAMINATIONS
Thermal tests

CONTACT
MY Studio
150 Lincoln Street, 3A
Boston, MA 02111
Tel: 617-517-4101
www.mystudio.us
my@mystudio.us

CONTINUOUSLY MORPHABLE CURVED SURFACES

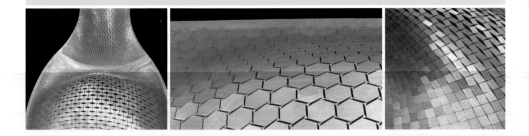

XURF (eXpandable sURFaces) Systems generates continuously morphable curved surfaces. Inspired by biological membranes, the resulting surfaces are rigid yet pliable and are able to respond to a variety of surfacing needs. Developed by Milgo/Bufkin, XURF allows the transformation of any flat-sheet material into a three-dimensionally curved surface and can accomplish compound curvature with relative ease. Applications include interior and exterior architectural surfaces, structures, sculpture, and a variety of design products. Milgo/Bufkin has developed prototypes primarily using steel, which range from containers and lamps to structural ceiling and wall systems.

CONTENTS
Metals or other sheet materials

APPLICATIONS
Architectural exterior and interior elements and surfaces

TYPES / SIZES
Custom

ENVIRONMENTAL
Substantial material efficiency in manufacturing surfaces with compound curvatures

TESTS / EXAMINATIONS
Full-scale prototypes

CONTACT
Milgo/Bufkin
68 Lombardy Street
Brooklyn, NY 11222
Tel: 718-388-6476
www.milgo-bufkin.com
milgomail@aol.com

MULTIDIMENSIONAL PROCESS

INDEX

DESIGNER INDEX

MANUFACTURER INDEX

PRODUCT INDEX